ADVANCE PRAISE FOR

T* IS FOR THRIVING:

Blueprints for Affirming Trans* and Gender Creative Lives and Learning in Schools

"*T* Is for Thriving* is a delightfully thoughtful and affirming book filled with meaningful lessons that assist students with self-reflection and self-awareness. Multi-stepped and intersectional lessons utilize strong literature-based learning experiences that naturally lend themselves to in-depth writing and creative experiences. Students will experience a stronger sense of self, belonging, and connectedness knowing that their feelings are inherently valued and supported."

—C. Scott Miller, Co-Chair
CTA LGBTQ+ Caucus, California Teacher Association
National Educators Association

"Through the gifts of practical wisdom, personal narratives, and innovative lesson plans, this beautiful, hopeful book simultaneously asserts the fundamental right of all children to a liberating education, and offers tangible strategies to get there."

—Dr. Yolanda Sealey-Ruiz
Professor of English Education
Teachers College, Columbia University

"Leading with joy, hope, and possibility, this collection of essays, reflections, and blueprints provide both theoretical and practical foundations for how to work alongside trans* and gender creative youth in ways that affirm dignity and agency. A highly-recommended read for educators, researchers, and organizers who look to co-design speculative, thriving queer futures inside and outside of the classroom."

—Dr. José R. Lizárraga
Assistant Professor
University of Colorado Boulder

"Though often well-intentioned, many advocates for trans* and gender creative youth rely on victimization narratives that reinscribe transphobic misery. This book foregrounds the agency, joy, and thriving of trans* and gender creative youth as tangible outcomes of our educational practice. For those of us in K-12 schools and teacher education, I hope that *T* Is for Thriving* becomes our mantra."

—Dr. Ed Brockenbrough
Associate Professor
University of Pennsylvania

"I am excited about this collection of first person narratives and educational resources that center the voices and lived experiences of trans* and gender creative students. This book gives the reader hope, nurtures understanding, and celebrates T*GC students. The volume includes lesson plans, situated in three theoretical frameworks, that provide readily applicable tools for educators to use in the classroom to spark self-love, joy and thriving among students. I highly recommend this compendium for all educators seeking to create inclusive schools for young people."

—Dr. Shireen Pavri
Assistant Vice Chancellor Educator & Leadership Programs
The California State University

"Queerly leaning scholars have paved ways for the arrival of Darling-Hammond's and Evans-Santiago's' collection of life-affirming and timely lessons. These "brave" lessons do not fear "covering" nor do they tiptoe or shy "around" topics that may land a teacher in jail or even have their teaching credentials revoked. NO! The collection of these life-affirming lessons makes an unapologetically urgent call to administrators, staff, teachers, families, and students to band and stand together to resist the nefarious and nonsensical patchwork of politics and to insist that all T*GC students deserve and are entitled to the same human rights as those of their peers. *Perhaps* one day we won't have to call queer scholarship or practitioner-research "brave," *then* one day we can stop endnoting, footnoting, or hash tagging a T*GC student's identity, and *finally*, thriving will manifest as it was always meant to be—for *all* students."

—Dr. sj Miller
Professor, Santa Fe Community College
Owner of DEIAB+ Consulting

"Nurtured from a profound love, this book is a rallying call for every one of us to create spaces for liberation grounded in radical care, safety, vulnerability, and hope. With a beautiful blend of theory, storytelling, and practice, this book is insightful, critical, and pragmatic in its steadfast invitation to create today the realities desperately needed to ensure we move past survival into thriving."

—Lucy Recio
Movement builder,
facilitator, and professor

T* IS FOR THRIVING

T* IS FOR THRIVING

Blueprints for Affirming Trans* and Gender Creative Lives and Learning in Schools

EDITED BY
KIA DARLING-HAMMOND AND BRE EVANS-SANTIAGO
FOREWORD BY SHAROON NEGRETE GONZÁLEZ

GORHAM, MAINE

Copyright © 2024 | Myers Education Press, LLC

Published by Myers Education Press, LLC
P.O. Box 424
Gorham, ME 04038

All rights reserved. No part of this book may be reprinted or reproduced in any form or by any electronic, mechanical, or other means, now known or hereafter invented, including photocopying, recording, and information storage and retrieval, without permission in writing from the publisher.

Myers Education Press is an academic publisher specializing in books, e-books, and digital content in the field of education. All of our books are subjected to a rigorous peer review process and produced in compliance with the standards of the Council on Library and Information Resources.

Library of Congress Cataloging-in-Publication Data available from Library of Congress.

13-digit ISBN 978-1-9755-0527-1 (paperback)
13-digit ISBN 978-1-9755-0528-8 (library networkable e-edition)
13-digit ISBN 978-1-9755-0529-5 (consumer e-edition)

Printed in the United States of America.

All first editions printed on acid-free paper that meets the American National Standards Institute Z39-48 standard.

Books published by Myers Education Press may be purchased at special quantity discount rates for groups, workshops, training organizations, and classroom usage. Please call our customer service department at 1-800-232-0223 for details.

Cover design by Kia Darling-Hammond and Teresa Lagrange
Cover art by Sophia Bertotti Metoyer

Visit us on the web at **www.myersedpress.com** to browse our complete list of titles.

For Bobbi and all those whose wholeness and possibility deserve the space to thrive.

CONTENTS

Acknowledgments	xi
Preface	xiii
Foreword	xvii
Introduction: Hope and Possibility for the Work of Trans* and Gender Creative Thriving	1

Part One — 17

TRANSformational Lotus: A Haiku — 18

1. Exploring and Reclaiming Home in Our Bodies — 19
   K. Elliott

2. Brain Chemicals and Kindness — 31
   Bre Evans-Santiago

3. Who Are You?: A Black Queer Journey to Selfhood and Community — 39
   Danelle Adeniji and DeKeisha Smith

4. Annie's Plaid Shirt — 51
   Wendy Garay and Bethany Gonzales

Interlude One — 59

5. Be You! — 61
   Ana Cornejo

6. Exploring Identity and Selfhood — 69
   Shaylyn Marks

Interlude Two
   What Are You Waiting For?: A Short Story — 81
   El Chen

Part Two — 85

7. Two-Spirit People and the Impact of Colonialism in California — 87
   Olivia Garrison

Interlude Three — 95

8. Female Husbands — 97
   Jada Thompson, Jay Wang, and Carol Jacob

Interlude Four — 107

9. Queering Counter-Narratives — 109
   Benjamin C. Kennedy and Alex Rosado-Torres

10. Yassifying Math With "The Hips on the Drag Queen" — 119
    El Chen with Cathery Yeh and B. E. Waid

11. 2SLGBTQIA+ Community Centers: A Beacon of Hope — 127
    B. E. Waid and Tyrone Martinez-Black

Conclusion — 141

Afterword — 145

Appendix A: Story Contributor Biographies — 149

Appendix B: Teaching Routines, Scaffolds, and Tools — 153

Appendix C: Editor Recommendations for Further Learning and Exploration — 157

About the Authors — 171

Index — 177

ACKNOWLEDGMENTS

My eternal gratitude to my T*GC niblings and siblings for anchoring me into this work and being my North Star. And to all of my students, who never cease to invite me to grow, laugh, and freedom dream. Thank you.

I am incredibly lucky to belong to my family of origin. Thank you for all the ways you've shown support, from reading drafts to sharing resources to feeding me real food to simply being an ear or a shoulder, as the situation required. I am likewise blessed by my chosen family without whom I simply would not exist. These past years have been particularly treacherous and all of you have buoyed me through (so many) long days, sleepless nights, emergencies, procedures, and tests. It puts everything into perspective. Thank you. I love you.

Bre and Sharoon – what a journey! Bre, thank you for inviting me into this powerful project. Sharoon, I'm thrilled by the myriad ways the fates connect us, which made this collaboration possible. Without you there would be no book. Thank you.

Finally, to our contributors—what you have done here is extraordinary. Generous. Courageous. Absolutely brilliant. Thank you for the gifts of your stories, your partnership, and your lessons. I am so excited for educators and young people everywhere to learn from you. Asé.

– Kia Darling-Hammond

I would like to thank my spouse, Bobbi, for not only inspiring me to move forward with this book, but also for your patience and support as the project developed. I see you, and I love you. To all of my kids that I have cared for in the past 18 years—my queer and unique children—I love you more than you know, and you are always my wings to pull me up and keep me going. A special shout-out to two amazing CSU Bakersfield Volleyball athletes who worked for me to help make this book come alive: Hana Makonova for her organization and special skills that helped finalize this project, and to Sophia Bertotti Metoyer for an amazing book cover. The world is lucky to have such amazing women in it, and I can't wait to see all of the amazing things you will achieve as you live your lives. A special shout-out to my friends and family for believing in my work and not only supporting me as a queer person, but also advocating with and for me when this country continues to push us down. Lastly, I must acknowledge and send all the hugs possible to this amazing editorial team. Kia and Sharoon, your love and vision for this book has made it come alive. Thank you for teaching me so many things throughout this journey, and I love you both to the moon and back. You are irreplaceable and phenomenal people! You make this world a better place with your energy and love.

– Bre Evans-Santiago

I would like to begin by expressing my heartfelt gratitude to all of the incredible educators who tirelessly nurture a sense of community and resilience within their classrooms, fueled by their unwavering love and care. A special tribute is owed to my dedicated colleagues through the years, whose remarkable ability to harmonize curricular demands with concern for the dignity of their students serves as a constant inspiration. I am deeply indebted to all the teachers who have played pivotal roles in my life, with a special place in my heart for my queer teachers. Through their profound scholarship, candid side chats, shared tea breaks, and significant academic and material support, they helped me believe in a hopeful and tangible queer future. To my biological and chosen family for their love and unconditional support to pursue what I am passionate about. My endless gratitude to Kia for inviting me to this project, hyping me up, mentoring me, and appreciating my endless bad jokes. To Bre, thank you for trusting me during this project and for teaching me to see myself as a scholar who has much to bring to the table. Finally, I am deeply indebted to all of the incredible contributors. This book, like their own schools and communities, has been immeasurably enriched by their presence.

– Sharoon Negrete González

PREFACE

THE IDEA TO WRITE this book grew from Bre's love for her spouse, Bobbi, his story, and Bre's work on LGBTQ+/SGL inclusion and education. As the idea took shape, Bre invited Kia to collaborate, anchoring the project in Kia's work on education, civil rights, and LGBTQ+/SGL thriving. A chance conversation with researcher Sharoon Negrete González turned the project duo into a trio and this volume came to life. In addition to the 18 lesson designers and 13 storytellers, our research and editing team comes to this work from a variety of vantage points:

Kia Darling-Hammond, Co-Editor

My proudest identity is "Auntie." Some of my niblings have also affectionately dubbed me "Buntie," "Cxntie," and "Queen Petty," to my everlasting delight. Nothing has affirmed me like being chosen by the young people in my life. It is my multigenerational chosen family that has revealed me to myself most clearly. I was a queer Black child who cosplayed a cis-hetero teenager and young adult with all the success of a fish trying to walk on land. The person I am today was given the space to breathe and become because I found a community that was unapologetic, out, and brave.

I come to the work we present here from several perspectives. I'll name just a few. In addition to my role as a community elder and nurturer, I am (still) Black and quite queer: a demi-pansexual with asexual tendencies living a gender identity somewhere at the intersection of aerogender, autismgender, and some other ways of existing that some young creatives will articulate somewhere on the internet (and likely already have).[1] I am a former teacher and school administrator, and a researcher who does teacher- and researcher-education work. This mission to provide trans* and gender-creative students the developmental opportunities they deserve *through* education bridges my personal and professional worlds.

I do this work for the ones who came before, for past little me and the inner child who remains, and for the precious beings who are navigating school now, as well as those who will come after them. I am doing this work to write the future they need into existence even as oppressive flames lick my feet. I hope you will join me.

Bre Evans-Santiago, Co-Editor

I identify as a Black, queer, pansexual, cis-gender woman. I value each of these identities and the intersections that elevate yet complicate who I am as a person. I also feel it is important to validate my big-bodiedness and disability. My limbs work but have been repaired and torn through my athletic life (over 25 years in sports). Lastly, I recognize that I am an unconventional mother and educator. Every single one of these identities is with me every day and affects my decisions in various aspects.

My spouse and I have been together for 16 years. Our relationship began as a lesbian couple, and later transformed to a pansexual couple. He was a part of my journey and I was a part of his as we learned about our trans* and gender-creative (T*GC) communities.

I have always been an advocate for and worked with LGBTQ youth as an educator. I learned so much from all of my "chilren" and I became more and more passionate for human rights and belonging as time progressed. I first encountered trans* and gender-creative folx when I played football for the Women's Football Alliance and the International Women's Football League. When some of my teammates and I became close and they stepped away from the sport due to sports regulations, I learned about transitioning, severe depression associated with gender dysphoria, and the processes it takes to legally change name and gender identities. Later in my life, I mentored, loved, supported, and validated several youth in various schools and colleges I worked for. Currently, as an educator and advisor for the youth organization and chair for the LGBTQ+ Faculty and Staff Affinity Group, we advocated for and provided safe spaces here at CSU Bakersfield.

I say this because my spouse, Bobbi, transitioned later in his life. First, I would like to say I think I was more excited than him when he told me because I felt like he was constantly trying to "fit" into a box he didn't feel good in. Then I asked him "Why now?" His response crushed my soul for a brief moment. His response was, "I didn't know people like me existed." So, because of our circle of amazing friends, he was able to see his true self.

As he went through his physical, mental, and legal identity transitions, I had another question, "What did your teachers say about trans* and gender-creative people?" He said, "no one ever talked about it. I just thought I was a lesbian who liked to dress like a 'boy' and do 'guy' stuff." That comment is why I chose to do this book. We have teacher allies who want to support but may not know where to start. We have teacher allies who need to learn more about what trans* and gender-creative youth need to thrive in schools. So, to me, this book is necessary.

Sharoon Negrete González, Researcher

I'll begin this section by clarifying how to pronounce my name because many people wonder after reading it for the first time. My name is Sharoon (*SHAH-rawn*). I am a queer, gender-fluid/nonbinary person of Otomí (Hñahñú) descent. I grew up in a housing project on the outskirts of Mexico City and attended school as a scholarship kid with experiences very distinct from those of my peers. I work today at the Folk Arts - Cultural Treasures Charter School (FACTS), an incredible institution that centers culturally competent education in Philadelphia's Chinatown.

I joined this project because I believe that we all deserve access to education that recognizes, empowers, and liberates us. I am convinced that we are in a pivotal moment and cannot delay in organizing and acting to protect our community—especially our youth. As we write this book, I can't help but think of my grandfather, Enrique González Ceballos, who passed away like so many others during what we now know as the AIDS Crisis. Then as now, our communities are confronted by existential threats in the form of state-sanctioned violence, unbridled hatred, and brute indifference. Then as now, we've got each other's backs. I trust that our courage, creativity, joy, hope, and strength will move us forward. I hope that this book will be useful to our community in this endeavor.

How the Book Was Made

Guided by a vision of creating with young Bobbi, and children like he was, in mind, we knew that we had to center *affirmation*. As a child in school, Bobbi didn't have models that reflected him back to himself in his wholeness. He didn't know that people like him existed. His self-actualization was delayed in ways many of his peers would never experience. We dream of a world where young people get to know and be supported as who they truly and fully are—not just so they can have developmentally robust childhoods, but also so they can experience thriving across their lifespan. Part of the formula for that affirmation is a young person having their developmental needs honored and met, or being in a *responsive* environment. For T*GC students, that includes being able to take care of their bodies by, for example, safely using a restroom they always have access to or halting a dysphoric pubertal experience or having the language and information to understand how they are changing and how to stay safe; it includes being provided with an array of positive role models—both live and historical—as well as having access to a rich, complex historical record that includes people like them; it includes being referred to by their claimed names and pronouns; and it includes an unwavering commitment to upholding their human and civil rights. Periodt.

Because T*GC folks are among those most targeted for abuse and erasure in our society, there is a lot about meeting young people's needs that lies in the realm of protection and activism and struggle. We are absolutely in a fight for their lives (and our own, truth be told). However, our young people need and deserve to feel joy! They deserve to be (and to see their communities) *celebrated* for who they are and all that they bring into any space. Celebrating could happen through visuals in the classroom, stories, music, and performances, and anything else we can do to cheer, clap, snap, and smile when referencing T*GC people in our world. It is that energy that sustains and inspires during a long fight for freedom.

When we decided to take contributions for this book, we particularly sought expertise from the T*GC community and asked our lesson designers and storytellers to think deeply about education that is affirming, responsive, *and* celebratory for T*GC students. In alignment with those three guiding principles, we also invited our lesson designers to ground their work in *gender complexity* (using sj Miller's Gender Identity Complexities Framework), *T*GC historical literacy* (adapting Gholdy Muhammad's Historically Responsive Literacy Framework), and the *right to thrive* (using Kia Darling-Hammond's Bridge to Thriving Framework). We discuss the frameworks in greater detail in our Introduction.

Ultimately, 18 authors shared their expertise in various content areas by creating inclusive lessons for our book. We had both individual and team submissions that showcase love, care, and a true breadth of knowledge throughout the text. Additionally, 13 beautiful individuals shared their stories with us, which we hope will inspire both compassion and action from our readers. We hope that our contributors' love and advocacy shine brightly from beginning to end.

This book's design was inspired by Gholdy Muhammad's presentation of her HRL framework in the delightful and highly usable book *Cultivating Genius* (2020). Following her lead, we worked to create a text that educators could "plug-and-play," something they could use easily and immediately.

A Note About the Title

When our publisher first asked us to use the word "blueprint," Bre actually cringed at the thought that readers might think we were advancing a single, unilateral "way" of "doing" this work. She didn't want to inform our readers that this is *the* solution because there are so many people that have also shared or will share ideas, strategies, and other blueprints. The lessons provided here are not the only way to teach, and this book is not the only text on this topic. Instead, this book is intended to provide strategies, suggestions, and ideas that educators can use right now. Part of what is so valuable about this text is that the lessons were predominantly written by T*GC and LGBQ+ folks. These are the voices of the community, and this text has not only provided a platform for their work but is also providing allies with guidance they can use immediately, today.

Notes

1. One wonderful resource for exploring a vast array of gender identities is Nonbinary Wiki (https://nonbinary.wiki/wiki/Main_Page)

FOREWORD

Sharoon Negrete González

Dear Reader, It is with great pleasure that I invite you into this book, a collection of community stories and lesson plans to assist educators designing responsive, celebratory, and affirming experiences for trans* and gender-creative (T*GC) students. The book is a response to the pressing need to address the gaps in educational practices and policies that have left T*GC students overlooked, underserved, and too often harmed. The consequences of these gaps can be dire, with T*GC youth overrepresented among those who drop out of school, are unhoused, consider self-harm, and are victimized and incarcerated.[1]

In recent years, we have witnessed an upsurge in violence against trans* people and increased discrimination, harassment, and murder.[2] Far-right organizations and politicians have promoted an anti-trans agenda, spreading disinformation and cruel rhetoric against trans* people.[3] This political climate heightens the urgency of the work in this book, as it is crucial to equip educators with the tools to create safe and inclusive spaces for T*GC students. This book highlights the efforts of educators, students, and community members to construct schools that neither erase T*GC students nor, as Beauchamp and D'Harlingue (2012) put it, use them as "tools for teaching," but instead allow "all students—both transgender and nontransgender—to articulate a range of understandings of their bodies and genders."[4]

As T*GC people continue to face violence, discrimination, and marginalization, it is crucial to recognize the interconnectedness of these issues with other forms of oppression. Susan Stryker, a trans* scholar and activist, notes in *Transgender History* (2008), "my own vision of a transgender social justice movement is one that addresses the specific kinds of problems transgender people can face in the world, by seeing them as structurally related to problems of racism, poverty, and other systemic injustices."[5] The struggle for trans* liberation must, therefore, be a collaborative and intersectional effort. Social justice requires trans* rights and liberation: the creation of a society that embraces gender diversity beyond binaries.

Settler colonialism, the ongoing project of anti-Indigenous genocide, and white supremacy, the enduring structures of dispossession and violence against people of color, have disproportionately impacted T*GC people from marginalized communities. But Black and Indigenous resistance and rebellion also provide us with models to imagine what comes next. As we navigate the current political climate, we can draw inspiration from Indigenous futurisms and Afrofuturisms to remain grounded and hopeful. Indigenous futurisms challenge settler colonialism by centering Indigenous perspectives and storytelling, creating visions of Indigenous liberation and decolonization. In the same way, Afrofuturism challenges white supremacy by centering Black experiences and creating alternative futures where Black people thrive. These frameworks offer a way to reject the panic and paralysis that the current political climate invites. Yet, despite these challenges, our community has shown remarkable resilience and strength. "Perhaps it's time to begin laying the groundwork for the next transformation," writes trans* scholar and activist Sandy Stone in *The Empire Strikes Back: A Posttranssexual Manifesto*. "Needless to say, however, beginnings are most delicate and critical periods in which, while the foundation stones are still exposed, it is necessary to pay exquisite attention to detail."[6]

Envisioning futures from the perspective of the oppressed allows us to center thriving, build initiative beyond defensive struggles, and imagine a future where trans* people can live without fear of violence or discrimination. This book represents a contribution to this approach, bearing testament to the vision, resilience, and strength of our community as we embody life as the ability "to stretch beyond the parameters of language, categories, binaries."[7]

To move towards this future, we must center the voices and leadership of T*GC people. We must engage in concrete action to support trans*-led organizations and advocate for trans*-affirming policies that address the intersecting forms of oppression that trans* and gender-creative people face. We must shape all of the spaces we have as safe and inclusive spaces, for in this moment of rising economic polarization and xenophobia, together with an unfolding climate crisis, we need to envision radical and extraordinary possibilities more than ever before.

As you engage with this book, I encourage you to reflect on your role in the T*GC struggle for liberation and the work of creating a world where we are recognized and celebrated for who we are. How can you utilize care, advocacy, affirmation, and celebration to create a more just and equitable world for T*GC students? How can you be a participant in transformative social change, empowering others to create spaces where T*GC students can thrive?

Notes

1. Abramovich, 2017; Cochran et al., 2002; Durso & Gates, 2012; Flentje et al., 2016; GLSEN, 2016; Shelton, 2016; Van Leeuwen et al., 2006
2. Ceron, 2023; Moeder, 2022
3. Jones & Huang, 2023; Rodriguez, 2023
4. Beauchamp and D'Harlingue, 2012, p. 36
5. Stryker, 2008, p. viii
6. Stone, 1992, p. 168
7. Menon, 2022

References

Abramovich, A. (2017). Understanding how policy and culture create oppressive conditions for LGBTQ2S youth in the shelter system. *Journal of Homosexuality, 64*(11), 1484–1501.

Beauchamp, T., & D'Harlingue, B. (2012). Beyond additions and exceptions: The category of transgender and new pedagogical approaches for Women's studies. *Feminist Formations, 24*(2), 25–51. https://doi.org/10.1353/ff.2012.0020

Ceron, E. (2023, March 8). 2023 is already a record year for Anti-LGBTQ bills in the US. *Bloomberg.com*. https://www.bloomberg.com/news/articles/2023-03-08/2023-is-already-a-record-year-for-anti-lgbtq-bills-in-the-us

Cochran, B. N., Stewart, A. J., Ginzler, J. A., & Cauce, A. M. (2002). Challenges faced by homeless sexual minorities: Comparison of gay, lesbian, bisexual, and transgender homeless adolescents with their heterosexual counterparts. *American Journal of Public Health, 92*(5), 773–777.

Durso, L. E, & Gates, G. J. (2012). Serving our youth: Findings from a national survey of services providers working with lesbian, gay, bisexual and transgender youth who are homeless or at risk of becoming homeless. *UCLA: The Williams Institute.* Retrieved from https://escholarship.org/uc/item/80x75033

Flentje, A., Leon, A., Carrico, A., Zheng, D., & Dilley, J. (2016). Mental and physical health among homeless sexual and gender minorities in a major urban US city. *Journal of Urban Health, 93*, 997–1009.

GLSEN. (2016). *Educational exclusion: Drop out, push out, and school-to-prison pipeline among LGBTQ youth.* New York: GLSEN.

Jones, I., & Huang, M. (2023, March 31). *On Trans Day of Visibility, we must fight anti-trans disinformation.* Newsweek. https://www.newsweek.com/trans-day-visibility-we-must-fight-anti-trans-disinformation-opinion-1791609

Menon, A. V. (2022, January 2). *Always becoming* [Blog post]. Retrieved from https://www.alokvmenon.com/blog/2022/1/2/always-becoming

Moeder, N. (2022, October 12). *Number of trans homicides doubled over 4 years, with gun killings fueling increase: Advocates.* ABC News. https://abcnews.go.com/US/homicide-rate-trans-people-doubled-gun-killings-fueling/story?id=91348274

Rodriguez, M. (2023, March 6). *CPAC Speaker Michael Knowles says "transgenderism must be eradicated."* Them. https://www.them.us/story/michael-knowles-transgenderism-cpac

Shelton, J. (2016). Reframing risk for transgender and gender-expansive young people experiencing homelessness. *Journal of Gay & Lesbian Social Services, 28*(4), 277–291.

Stone, S. (1992). The empire strikes back: A posttranssexual manifesto. *Camera Obscura, 10*(2 (29)), 150–176. https://doi.org/10.1215/02705346-10-2_29-150

Stryker, S. (2008). *Transgender history.* Seal Press.

Van Leeuwen, J. M., Boyle, S., Salomonsen-Sautel, S., Baker, D. N., Garcia, J. T., Hoffman, A., & Hopfer, C. J. (2006). Lesbian, gay, and bisexual homeless youth: An eight-city public health perspective. *Child Welfare*, 151–170.

INTRODUCTION

Hope and Possibility for the Work of Trans* and Gender Creative Thriving

THIS EDITED VOLUME IS a contribution to the rich existing scholarship about meeting trans* and gender-creative students' needs in schools. The project is focused on hope and possibility and seeks to amplify community-grounded guidance about being *responsive* to students in ways that are not just *affirming*, but also *celebratory*. This is a text for world-making.[1] This is a revolutionary text.

What Do We Mean by Trans* and Gender Creative?

Scholar sj Miller, whose work stands as a pillar of inspiration for this project, provides this foundation for understanding what "trans* and gender creative," or T*GC, means:

> Trans* [is] a prefix or adjective used as an abbreviation of transgender ... Many consider trans* to be an inclusive and useful umbrella term. Trans (without the asterisk) is most often applied to trans men and trans women, and the asterisk is used more broadly to refer to all non-cisgender gender identities, such as (a)gender, cross-dresser, bigender, genderfluid, gender**k, genderless, genderqueer, nonbinary, non-gender, third gender, trans man, trans woman, transgender, transsexual, and two-spirit. [Gender creative can be defined as] expressing gender in a way that demonstrates individual freedom of expression and that does not conform to any gender.[2]

Why A Pedagogy for Trans* and Gender Creative Students?

"We need pedagogies that concentrate more of our efforts on inviting people to be with each other in our full humanity. We need pedagogies that deeply examine how

our current gender system confines us all and how that interacts with other systems, like race, class, and ability. We need pedagogies that aim toward the immediately necessary projects of preventing the murders and suicides of trans people in addition to preventing our slower deaths at the hands of inadequate medical and legal systems. We need pedagogies that listen to transgender experience in all its forms."

— Harper B. Keenan[3]

We have inherited a world full of constraints. "Our culture today," writes historian Susan Stryker, "tries to reduce the wide range of livable body types to two and only two genders, one of which is subject to greater social control than the other."[4] She points out that "when we come into the world, somebody else tells us who they think we are. [. . .] They determine our sex and assign us a gender. We come into self-awareness and grow up in the context created for us by these meanings and decisions, which predate our individual existence."[5] And it continues where, "from the moment they start preschool or kindergarten, children are socialized to conform to their teachers' expectations for good behavior and how to appropriately dress, play, and act according to their perceived gender role."[6]

Like the society they inhabit, schools reflect practices of gender policing and surveillance where nonconforming students are punished, excluded, and harmed—their learning disrupted.[7] But, Stryker points out that the reality is that

> . . . Both gender and sex can be understood in nonbinary ways, [so] it's more productive to ask *how* somebody is cis (that is, how different aspects of their bodies and minds line up on the side of gender divisions in privileged ways) and *how* they are trans (that is, how they cross the boundaries of their birth-assigned gender in ways that can have adverse social consequences) and to recognize that all people, however they are cis or trans, are subjected to nonconsensual social gendering practices that privilege some and discriminate against others.[8]

In Melinda Mangin's (2020) study, one educator reflected on the insight that a single question about gender could elicit, sharing, "The Transgender Alliance came and . . . the first question they asked us was, 'When did you decide you were a girl or a boy?' . . . That question was so great because nobody decides. . . . Everybody says, 'I just knew.'"[9] Not only did the responses suggest the ubiquity of social norming around gender, but also that each person can have a deep, embodied capacity to simply know what is true about their gender.

As foundational scholar Cris Mayo notes,

> Young trans people are coming out earlier and more often. Our task is to ensure that they are met with care and recognition of their complex work with and through genders, and to ensure they have access to educational contexts that encourage their

flourishing, their creativity, and their potential to continue to help us all to think, read, and live gender better.[10]

How young trans* and gender-creative people exist in the world can be a beacon to guide us toward greater imagination and freedom, but only if we make it safe. That is what they need and it's what they deserve. Pedagogies that embrace the full scope and possibility of humanity include all children. They do this because belonging is necessary for healthy development and because it is just. The stakes are, indeed, life and death.

We can't allow ourselves to be lulled into inaction by the increased positive visibility of T*GC communities in popular culture (including films, novels, ad campaigns, and more) and the few civil rights advances of the recent past,[11] because "heightened visibility has also come with increased transphobic rhetoric and sentiment."[12] Furthermore, T*GC youth experience particularly "hostile school climates, and report more negative experiences than their cisgender LGBQ peers," suffering discrimination and violence that "contribute to poor academic outcomes," increase their "risk for poor physical and mental health," and prevent them from equitably "accessing educational environments in the same capacity as other youth."[13] Melinda Mangin (2020) cites developmental psychologist Kristina Olson when noting that "transgender adolescents and adults suffer elevated risk of anxiety, depression, and suicidality as a result of rejection, stigma, prejudice, and discrimination."[14]

Thankfully, there is wisdom to guide improving T*GC student experiences. Clark et al. (2022) note the power of "supportive educators, inclusive and enumerated school policies, LGBTQ-inclusive curriculum, and Gender and Sexuality Alliances (GSAs)."[15] Meyer, Regan, and Jenkins (2022) offer additional guidance about creating affirming learning environments through transpedagogies, like that described by Harper B. Keenan above, and gender-expansive classroom practices, like inclusive book selection. Finally, Melinda Mangin (2020) has crafted an entire book about creating an affirming and inclusive culture for transgender students, tapping into the experiences of educators who have actually done the work. She identifies the following elements:

1. Supportive principals who position themselves as lead learners, employ an individual child-centered approach (seeing children as unique individuals with specific needs), and foster strong school–family collaboration, while providing school support in the absence of family support.
2. Educators who leverage a commitment "to lifelong professional learning [that] embraces the growing visibility of transgender students as a potential learning opportunity." In the book she delves into how practitioners answered the question "Who needs to know what, and why?" as well as some creative approaches to providing professional development and community learning.

3. Gender-inclusive classroom practices. Foremost, with a focus on students' social-emotional well-being and their sense of belonging to the larger community, that affirms their "varied ways of being, their complex histories, and their multiple identities," including gender identity and expression, and classroom instruction that decreases gendered practices and increases discussions about gender.
4. Addressing gendered school spaces—with possibilities (depending on setting) for accommodating transgender and gender-expansive students (i.e., safe alternative bathroom access), assimilating students (i.e., access to bathrooms and gendered activities aligned to gender identity), or modifying spaces for universal accessibility (not asking students to adapt to gendered spaces/activities, but rather changing spaces and activities to be accessible regardless of gender identity: gender-neutral bathrooms; nongendered activities like dances, etc.).
5. Reculturing schools for gender equity—Mangin points out that "school cultures continue to reproduce the gender norms that contribute to the dehumanization of transgender identities, even when individual children are affirmed and supported. . . . Actions meant to signal change such as 'safe school' stickers, rainbow flags, and anti-bullying posters remain largely symbolic in the absence of deeper cultural change. Changing educational practice is difficult under the best circumstances . . . [but] change *can* begin with individual educators [and] educators should not wait for individual transgender children to disclose their gender identity before engaging in the work necessary to shift gender norms, [as] gender-expansive and transgender children and those who are questioning their gender are already enrolled in our schools, even if they are not disclosed. . . . Binary gender norms constrain everyone." Mangin urges educators to be proactive about: making space for transgender and gender-expansive identities; inviting difficult conversations about gender; and developing formal policies and written curriculum.[16]

It's so important to underscore that there *are* T*GC young people in our schools, whether we know it or not. Adults, too. According to GLSEN's 2021 National School Climate Survey, in a sample of 22,209 students aged 13 to 21 living across all 50 U.S. states, DC, and the territories, 26.9% were transgender, 31.5% were nonbinary, and an additional 7.9% were questioning their gender (pp. 6-7). The UCLA School of Law's Williams Institute estimates that within the entire U.S. population, roughly 1.6 million people aged 13 and older are transgender as of 2022. Susan Stryker reminds us that these numbers are conservative estimates based on limited data, as not every trans* or gender creative person can or will disclose their identity on such surveys, and these values leave out all people under age 13.

As is the case for all marginalized communities, T*GC histories, contributions, triumphs, and brilliance must be spotlit, they must be *celebrated* and *affirmed*—not simply during designated months like Pride in June, when school is largely out of session, or LGBTQ+ History Month in October—but all year, across subjects, and beyond classrooms themselves. Meaningful inclusion raises awareness of the full scope of human existence, increasing a community's ability to meet its members' needs, undermining discrimination, and increasing the possibility of liberation.

Full inclusion aligns to what is real, and what is real is that trans* and gender creative people exist (and always have).[17] And that they are trans* and gender creative all day, every day.

As is true for all children, T*GC students need to see themselves robustly represented—their existence, their humanity, and their rights affirmed. They need to know they aren't alone, that they have a powerful lineage, that there are possibilities for them, and that they are whole and entitled to thrive.

Fundamentally, what it continues to come down to is that safe and inclusive schools see better student outcomes, higher teacher retention and satisfaction, and more stability all around. Punitive and exclusionary schools see the opposite.

Like Melinda Mangin, we believe that most educators want to support their students and see them thrive. As she points out, "what appears to be a lack of support for transgender students may stem from a lack of know-how, fear of reprisals, or worries about getting it right."[18] We urge you to try anyway, remembering that the stakes can't get higher.

For those educators who "question whether their limited time should be spent learning about transgender children," Mangin points out that "the real problem [is] rigid enforcement of binary gender norms [that have] a direct adverse effect on everyone because [they] limit who we can be and what we can do. [They] reinforce and perpetuate inequity."[19] In this time of legislative volatility, it can be difficult to know what's allowable. We recommend tuning in to the American Civil Liberties Union, the Human Rights Campaign, the Transgender Law Center, and GLSEN.

For readers seeking additional education and training focused on T*GC communities, including language that can be used to communicate about gender effectively, we recommend beginning with resources provided by Gender Spectrum, GLSEN, and the HRC Welcoming Schools program. And, of course, please read this book! Use the lessons our contributors have designed. Acknowledging that the world is hard right now, we are excited to present a text that offers counternarratives and celebrates T*GC genius and joy directly from the community.

Scholarly Lineage

As we present this contribution, we acknowledge that we are perched on the shoulders of brilliant scholars, some of whom we name here, and several of whom we do not. Above, we have brought in the words and works (in no particular order) of sj Miller, Marío Suárez, Susan Stryker, Cris Mayo, Melinda Mangin, Harper B. Keenan, Caitlin M. Clark, Joseph G. Kosciw, Padraig Hurley, Elizabeth J. Meyer, Page Valentine Regan, and Kelly Jenkins.

The scholarship is long standing and dynamic. By way of example, Cris Mayo has been calling our attention to these pressing issues in education for decades. In fact, almost 20 years ago, Cris highlighted the importance of Gay–Straight Alliances (GSAs), emphasizing the power in resistance and how GSAs provide safety and affirmation for community, identity, and allyship.[20]

Harper B. Keenan recently published an article with drag queen Lil Miss Hot Mess identifying five elements of Drag Queen Story Hour that invite early childhood educators into "a sense of queer imagination: play as praxis, aesthetic transformation, strategic defiance, destigmatization of shame, and embodied kinship." This drag pedagogy "provides a performative approach to queer pedagogy that is not simply about LGBT lives, but *living queerly*."[21]

Mario Suárez, who honored our project by penning its Afterword, works with numerous researchers in the field to reinforce the need for educators to learn about and from LGBTQ+ communities as they evolve their practice.[22] His co-edited text published with Melinda Mangin in 2022 houses chapters written by education practitioners and scholars on topics ranging from how to conduct ethical research, to the experiences of transgender students in school, to community programs, to educating teachers.

Sharon Verner Chappell, Karyl E. Ketchum, and Lisa Richardson published the popular, groundbreaking *Gender Diversity and LGBTQ Inclusion in K-12 Schools: A Guide to Supporting Students, Changing Lives* (2018), offering strategies and ideas for inclusion across grade levels, as well as a chart to support intentionally changing our language by "doing this, not that."

B.E. Waid, who contributed to this volume twice, is a pioneer in math education with LGBTQ+ youth. Their math camps, Instagram Live chats and interviews, educational videos, online curriculum, and publications make building an inclusive, powerful math practice accessible to educators and students alike.[23]

We are proud to add our work to the rich pool of scholarship that precedes and inspires it. We hope educators will see this as one of many tools available to them and that they will feel empowered to use it without hesitation.

As we have dug into the literature on this topic, we feel it is crucial to acknowledge that one of our most threatened communities, Black trans* women, is glaringly underrepresented among published scholars and educators. We know there are numerous reasons why Black trans* women might choose not to participate in this work, from simply having to focus on survival, to lack of sufficient compensation, to erasure and lack of access. There is a clear connection between what happens in society and experiences in K-12 schools and who finds their way into higher education and onto bookshelves. We are sending love to Black trans* girls and women as they navigate these incredibly trying, dangerous times. We see you and we are working to build the pathways you deserve.

Book Overview

We have split the book into two parts: a section on affirming selfhood and a section about affirming the community. Within each section are lesson plans and community stories designed to bring a responsive, affirming, and celebratory experience to life for trans* and gender-creative students.

> *"I think especially in the face of a really vitriolic, nasty media cycle... how do we continue to tell our own stories first? And if we can tell our own stories first and enough, there's a privilege and a burden of being out there, which is that you get to help people that you may never ever know about. That became very clear to me when I was doing that early visibility work in the 1990s. And it was back when AOL chat boards were the bleeding edge of technology. I would get messages from people saying, 'I really feel like you saved my life by telling your truth.' And it's that hearing your own story from someone else's life, and that healing that begins to happen, and realizing that you're not broken, and you're not alone. And you're okay. I didn't save anybody's life. You saved your own life, because you stepped up and said, 'This is me.'"* – M. Rice

The Stories

Through interviews, we invited T*GC community members to share their wisdom about what an affirming, celebratory, and responsive education for them and the larger community could include. It is no surprise that several major challenges were named, including rigid, binaristic gender norms and expectations, which remain common in schools.[24] Benjamin shared, "I felt like the characteristics of [traditional] masculinity in a Black man did not resonate with me . . . I don't see myself in that figure." Our storytellers also talked about bathroom access. El, for example, said, "Bathrooms were the main problem for me. I used to go to the girl's restroom, and I would get pushed out because they thought I was a boy. And other times, people would ask, 'Are you a boy or a girl?' And I'm actually nonbinary."

Most storytellers within this book also had some experience with gender affirmation, whether it was people honoring their pronouns, finding accessible bathrooms, or finding a supportive community. Their stories provide tangible evidence of what so many experience and need. Both the hardships and triumphs point toward what we *can* do and design to build the education that T*GC students require. Throughout the text, we highlight these community voices, weaving vignettes between and through the academic lessons to emphasize community wisdom. We are also lucky to be able to publish Bobbi Evans-Santiago's poem "TRANSformational Lotus" and El Chen's short story, "What Are You Waiting For?" as part of this volume. Brief storyteller biographies are in Appendix A.

The Lessons

This text is outlined to provide educators and allies the opportunity to intentionally include curricula across several content areas. The lessons are built to guide teachers at any level through and allow for immediate implementation. They closely follow the 5E model,[25] which provides a guide to scaffold high quality engagement and inquiry. Most of the lessons make use of handouts, materials, and resources, which readers can find cited in the chapter references, and instructional routines, scaffolds, and tools, which are linked in the chapters and in Appendix B. Digital resources are also online at https://www.tisforthriving.com/. Finally, we have offered Appendix C, with readings for further learning and exploration.

A Book in Two Parts

Part One: Affirming Selfhood

The first chapter, "Exploring and Reclaiming Home in Our Bodies," uses individual and collective reflection, storytelling, movement, and artistic expression to provide space for youth to explore the concept of "home" across multiple dimensions. The next chapter, "Brain Chemicals and Kindness," integrates science, math, and reading literature in order to provide a celebratory space for acts of kindness and how those acts affect our brains. The chapter "Who Are You?" uses reading, journaling, and reflection to help Black LGBTQ+ and same-gender-loving students critically reflect on their identities and the power of self-definition, as well as understand the significance of creating supportive, inclusive spaces for Black and other LGBTQ+/SGL individuals. The next three chapters, "Annie's Plaid Shirt," "Be You," and "Exploring Identity and Selfhood," are all Language Arts and reading lessons that incorporate embracing identity, gender exploration, and challenging gender roles in school and beyond.

Part Two: Affirming the Community

The lesson "Two-Spirit People and the Impact of Colonialism in California" challenges the Mission Project typically assigned in California schools by replacing it with a project that uplifts Indigenous voices, focuses on resistance, and centers Indigenous joy through creativity. "Female Husbands" raises awareness about the existence of female husbands and engages students in meaningful conversations about gender and gender roles in society, while "Queering Counter-Narratives" centers transgender history and the lived experiences of the T*GC community. The next chapter, "Yassifying Math with 'The Hips on the Drag Queen'" takes a celebratory approach to counting with drag queens. Finally, an advanced math lesson challenges us to look at community centers across states and what challenges or needs should be addressed in order to create "Beacons of Hope."

The Frameworks

As noted earlier, this volume is intended to provide a resource for educators and allies that enables responsive, affirming, and celebratory education for T*GC students. To guide lesson design, we pointed our contributors to three frameworks: sj Miller's *Gender Identity Complexities Framework*, Gholdy Muhammad's *Historically Responsive Literacy Framework*, and Kia Darling-Hammond's *Bridge to Thriving Framework*.[26] All three recognize the power of not only affirming student identity, but also applying a critical lens to both one's own work and the larger world.

Gender Identity Complexities Framework

The GICF is elaborated in sj Miller's 2019 book *About Gender Identity Justice in Schools and Communities*. Reminding us that our students' identities aren't immediately visible, Miller asks, "How do we learn to recognize what we don't even know we *should* know?"[27] The answer is, we have to unlearn the deeply embedded practice of assuming anything about any aspect of people's identities. We have to cultivate a practice of respectful curiosity.

Gender identity complexity is "the constant integration of new ideas and concepts and the invention of new knowledges—comprised of multitudes, and/or a moving away, or sometimes a refusal to accept historically conferred constructions of binaries, genders, and bodies. . . . Gender identity can be some of these, all of these, or none of these. It evades and resists categorization."[28]

The GICF "provides strategies for approaching the classroom, constructing lessons, and presenting possibilities for shifting educational . . . contexts and environments."[29] It is guided by a series of axioms and ten principles to inform design and advocacy. We encourage readers to explore Miller's text, as Miller provides examples of how to apply each principle and offers resources to support that work. We translated Miller's ten principles and their related commitments into guiding questions for our lesson contributors as follows:

Gender Complexity

1. How do you advocate for complex gender identities?
2. How do you demonstrate that gender and gender identity are fluid and can shift over time and across contexts?

Authenticity

3. How do you hold space for others to be who they are without ascribing a gender or gender identity to them?
4. How do you actively support various and multiple performances of gender and expressions of gender identity?

Self-Definition

5. How do you invite students to self-define or claim their gender, name, and/or pronouns?

Critical Consciousness

6. How do you provide opportunities for students to explore, engage, understand, and push back against gender and gender identity constructs?
7. How do you challenge gender and gender identity norms and stereotypes?
8. How do you attend to the ways that gender identities are influenced by social, historical, cultural, economic, religious, linguistic, and other forces, including age, body size, disability, national origin, and so on?
9. How do you create opportunities for students to be proactive change agents?

Historically Responsive Literacy Framework

Gholdy Muhammad's HRL Framework evolved from her study of 19th century Black literary societies. She noticed that "each time they came together to read, write, and think, they were making sense of who they were (identity), developing their proficiencies in the content they were learning within (skills), becoming smarter about something or gaining knowledge (intellect), and finally, developing the ability to read texts (including print and social contexts) to understand power, authority, and oppression (criticality).[30] She went on to note that "criticality is also related to seeing, naming, and interrogating the world not only to make sense of injustice but also to work toward social transformation. [. . .] Students need spaces to name and critique injustice and ultimately have the agency to build a better world."[31] As her framework took off, Muhammad added a fifth dimension: joy.

Centering marginalized students, Muhammad argues for "a reframed set of learning standards in literacy education [that are] grounded in history and [restore] excellence in education." These enable "educators to reimagine what learning can look like and begin to offer a promising framework for students who have not traditionally seen themselves in formal learning situations."[32] While Muhammad's focus is on Black children, the framework can be applied to T*GC children, some of whom are, of course, also Black.

HRL invites educators to reflect on a series of design questions along each of the framework's dimensions. They are:

1. **Identity:** How does our curriculum and instruction help students to learn something about themselves and/or about others? Identity learning should encompass anti-racist [and anti-oppression] approaches so that students learn the truth and excellence of marginalized communities.
2. **Skills:** How does our curriculum and instruction respond to or build students' skills in literacy [including] language arts?

3. **Intellect:** How does our curriculum and instruction respond to or build upon students' knowledge and mental powers? What are they becoming smarter about?
4. **Criticality:** How does our curriculum and instruction engage students' thinking about power, equity, and the disruption of oppression?
5. **Joy:** How does our curriculum and instruction elevate beauty, truth, and happiness in humanity?[33]

Bridge to Thriving Framework

Grounded in their work with secondary school students, then their doctoral research, Darling-Hammond's *Bridge to Thriving Framework* outlines six dimensions of thriving as described first by Black LGBTQ+ and same-gender-loving youth and young adults, then reinforced through work with other communities.[34] The framework is described as a bridge between hardship, survival, and scarcity on the one end, and wholeness, thriving, or the ability to "simply be" in one's fullness on the opposite end. It acknowledges that people realistically move back and forth between the two poles and that the thriving dimensions encompass practices, strategies, experiences, and tools they might use along the way.

As a framework that centers marginalized communities it stretches beyond resilience or integration into the current world. People experience thriving when they:

1. have supportive, affirming communities (often affinity community focused on applying critical consciousness to advancing social justice and equity) and feel a sense of true belonging (not just fitting in) [**Community**];
2. can come to know their true selves, love themselves, and self-assert in a self-determined and empowered way [**Selfhood**];
3. have not just economic stability but also abundant resources for thriving, including time, space, and—crucially—hope, aspirations, and dreams [**Abundance**];
4. can engage in pleasurable activities (with or without others), pursue their passions, and be joyful [**Pleasure**]; and
5. can heal and experience relief from stressors like unsafety, erasure, economic hardship, and social isolation [**Relief**], among others.
6. In particular, people describe an optimal state of thriving—one in which the first five dimensions tend to be activated together—as "**Simply Being**," or being able to exist fully and be whole.

The *Bridge to Thriving Framework* invites educators to reflect on the following questions along each of the model's six dimensions:

1. **Community:** How does your pedagogy and curriculum support conditions for each student to experience true belonging, affirmation, and critical consciousness?

2. **Selfhood:** How does your pedagogy and curriculum help students see and embrace their authentic selves in affirming, empowered, and self-determined ways?
3. **Abundance:** How does your pedagogy and curriculum provide opportunities for expansiveness, imagining, dreaming, creating, and building hope? How does your practice invite students to drive their learning experiences?
4. **Pleasure:** How does your pedagogy and curriculum leverage play, joy, pleasure, connection, and students' passions to cultivate learning?
5. **Relief:** How does your pedagogy and curriculum reduce or eliminate stressors like feelings of unsafety, scarcity, confinement, unfreedom, or illness? How does your design make rest, healing, and well-being possible?
6. **Simply Being:** How does your pedagogy and curriculum create conditions for wholeness—a sense that people can exist fully? How does your practice honor students holistically (mind, body, spirit, and heart)?

Meeting the Moment

"It would be remarkable if all the historic changes in how society understands and accepts trans and gender-nonconforming people failed to produce a backlash among people hostile to those changes"

— Susan Stryker[35]

For so many years it seems every day has brought news of disintegration in nearly every facet of our lives—our health, our schools, our homes, our governments, our planet, and on and on. Most heavily impacted are those of us who exist outside of the centered and celebrated group(s) in this hegemonic culture. Our communities are ignored, misrepresented, harmed, scapegoated, and disposed of. As a result, marginalized groups are left to advance their own, often corrective, efforts to make themselves visible and legible; to speak their truths; and to end their dehumanization at the hands of the state, their communities, and sometimes their own families. It's work that can't happen in hiding, so—highly exposed—T* GC folks are saddled with the burden of saving their own lives.

Dr. Martin Luther King, Jr. (1963) wrote, "Injustice anywhere is a threat to justice everywhere. We are caught in an inescapable network of mutuality, tied in a single garment of destiny. Whatever affects one directly, affects all indirectly." We are all implicated in these battles for not only the right to full participation in society, but, crucially, the right to full existence as human beings. This is a fight for possibility and a world we deserve, but it is also, urgently, a fight to save lives right now.

As scary as it can be when politicians and state legislatures work to silence dissenters, including teachers offering LGBTQ+-inclusive curriculum in their classrooms,[36] the fact remains that the only way to win is to refuse to be cowed. If you ever wondered what you would have done at the start of Germany's Nazi regime it's what you are doing now. This is that moment. Again.

INTRODUCTION

As we are finishing this text, the Human Rights Campaign has officially declared a "State of Emergency" for LGBTQ+ Americans.[37] Only four U.S. states mandate LGBTQ+-inclusive curricula, despite there being roughly 60 million LGBTQ+ individuals in the country. There have been more than 650 anti-LGBTQ+ bills introduced and currently 474 are being carefully tracked by the American Civil Liberties Union.[38] The numbers continue to climb throughout the country, and within these bills, nearly 200 directly target T*GC people, which affects both affirmation and accommodations in schools, medical care, and government recognition. Not all bills will pass, but with so many conservatives controlling decision-making bodies across the country, from school boards to Congress, our resistance needs to be louder.

Still, struggle is not the *only* story. Struggle doesn't provide enough fuel to persevere. For that we need possibility models, mutual aid, a politics of refusal, and joy. This book contributes in that regard: to make it easier for educators to be, as they historically have been, brave and defiant in the face of oppression. Here are stories to read and share. Here are lessons to teach or adapt. Here is some fuel to sustain us.

James Baldwin once said, "hope is invented every day,"[39] so here are some developments from just the past month (August 2023) to feed your hope:

- A Montana state court judge blocked a ban on gender affirming care for trans* youth.
- Kyne Santos is about to publish the book *Math in Drag*.
- The Harris County Public Library officially became a book sanctuary, fighting censorship and book bans.
- A federal judge declared Texas' drag ban unconstitutional.
- The State of Our Nation survey found that 83% of U.S. adults think politicians should stop targeting the T*GC community and 72% think they are too ill-informed about gender-affirming care for minors to create fair policies.
- Tennessee just elected Olivia Hill to public office, a historic first.
- California Governor Gavin Newsom signed a bill barring schoolbook bans based on racial and LGBTQ+ topics.
- California will begin recognizing August as Transgender History Month in 2024.

Though it may not be immediately obvious, people *are* moving liberation work forward everywhere every day. We will make faster progress the more people join the fight. To that end, a pedagogy that is responsive to trans* and gender creative students must be explicit, deliberate, courageous, and defiant. It must center T*GC people without apology. The larger society, particularly those with more safety and power, must become educated, unlearn limiting beliefs, bring narratives and perspectives into the spaces where they are absent, and leverage their relative safety to increase other people's freedom. This has always been the work.

We hope this book provides ease, support, and immediately actionable tools that educators can use to provide *responsive, affirming*, and *celebratory* learning environments for T*GC students. Thank you for your love, allyship, and willingness to act.

Notes

1. Zaino, 2021
2. Miller, 2019b, p. 18 notes 1 and 2
3. Keenan, 2017, p. 553
4. Stryker, 2017, p.17
5. Stryker, 2017, p. 12
6. Meyer, Regan, & Jenkins, 2022, p. 137
7. Mangin, 2020, p. 4
8. Stryker, 2017, pp. 12–13
9. Mangin, 2020, p. 74, emphasis added
10. In Miller 2019b, p. ix
11. "Litigation in eight states has repeatedly clarified that transgender and gender-expansive students should be treated in a manner consistent with their gender identity, under Title IX of the Education Amendments of 1972" (Mangin, 2020, pp. 61–62).
12. Clark, Kosciw, & Hurley, 2022, p. 72
13. Clark, Kosciw, & Hurley, 2022, p. 73
14. Mangin, 2020, p. 61
15. Clark, Kosciw, & Hurley, 2022, pp. 83–84
16. Mangin, 2020, p. 70, 100, 149
17. See Younes, 2018.
18. Mangin, 2020, p. 3
19. Mangin, 2020, pp. 3–4
20. Mayo, 2004
21. Keenan & Hot Mess, 2021, p. 440
22. Suárez et al., 2019
23. The Queer Mathematics Teacher, 2023
24. Evans-Santiago & Reinking, 2020
25. NASA.gov, 2023
26. Because these frameworks are referenced so frequently throughout the text, they are not cited every time they appear.
27. Miller, 2019a, p. 3
28. Miller, 2019a, p. 11
29. Miller, 2019a, p. 60
30. Muhammad, 2018, p. 138
31. ibid.
32. Muhammad, 2020, p. 11
33. Muhammad & Mosley, 2021, p. 194
34. Darling-Hammond, 2018 and Darling-Hammond, 2022
35. Stryker, 2017, p. 226
36. Evans-Santiago, Reinking, & Beck, 2023; Greytak & Kosciw, 2014
37. HRC, 2023
38. ACLU, 2023
39. Adelsen, 1970, p. 46

References

ACLU. (2023). Mapping attacks on LGBTQ rights in U.S. state legislatures. https://www.aclu.org/legislative-attacks-on-lgbtq-rights

Adelsen, C. E. (1970, March). "A love affair: James Baldwin and Istanbul." *Ebony Magazine*, 40–46. https://books.google.com/books?id=vtVJKRwRDLgC&lpg=PA1&pg=PA40#v=onepage&q&f=false

Chappell, S., Richardson, L., & Ketchum, K. (2018). *Gender diversity and LGBTQ inclusion in K-12 schools: A guide to supporting students, changing lives*. Routledge.

Clark, C. M., Kosciw, J. G., & Hurley, P. (2022). Life in school for transgender and nonbinary students: Student experiences and key supports. In M. I. Suárez & M. M. Mangin (Eds), *Trans studies in K-12 education: Creating an agenda for research and practice*. Harvard Education Press.

Darling-Hammond, K. (2018). *To simply be: Thriving as a Black queer/same-gender-loving young adult*. Stanford University.

Darling-Hammond, K. (2022, January 20). Dimensions of thriving: Learning from Black LGBTQ+/SGL moments, spaces, and practices. *Nonprofit Quarterly*. https://nonprofitquarterly.org/dimensions-of-thriving-learning-from-black-lgbtq-sgl-moments-spaces-and-practices/

Evans-Santiago, B., & Reinking, A. (2020). "Are you a boy or a girl?" In B. Evans-Santiago (Ed). *Mistakes we have made: Implications for social justice educators*. Myers Education Press

Evans-Santiago, B, Reinking, A, & Beck, B. (2023). California FAIR Act ten years later: Elementary teachers still uncomfortable with LGBTQ+ curriculum. *Issues in Teacher Education, 31*(3).

Greytak, E. A., & Kosciw, J. G. (2014). Predictors of US teachers' intervention in anti-les-bian, gay, bi-sexual, and transgender bullying and harassment. *Teaching Education, 25*(4), 410–426. https://doi.org/10.1080/10476210.2014.920000

HRC. (2023, June 6). For the first time ever, Human Rights Campaign officially declares 'State of Emergency' for LGBTQ+ Americans; Issues national warning and guidebook to ensure safety for LGBTQ+ residents and travelers. https://www.hrc.org/press-releases/for-the-first-time-ever-human-rights-campaign-officially-declares-state-of-emergency-for-lgbtq-americans-issues-national-warning-and-guidebook-to-ensure-safety-for-lgbtq-residents-and-travelers

Keenan, H. B. (2017). Unscripting curriculum: Toward a critical trans pedagogy. *Harvard Educational Review, 87*(4), 538–556.

Keenan, H. B., & Hot Mess, L. M. (2021). Drag pedagogy: The playful practice of queer imagination in early childhood. *Curriculum Inquiry, 50*(5), 440–461. https://doi.org/10.1080/03626784.2020.1864621

King Jr, M. L. (1963). Letter from the Birmingham Jail, April 16, 1963. *What Country Have I*, 125.

Mangin, M. M. (2020). *Transgender students in elementary school: Creating an affirming and inclusive school culture*. Harvard Education Press.

Mayo, C. (2004) Queering school communities. *Journal of Gay & Lesbian Issues in Education, 1*(3), 23–36. https://doi.org/10.1300/J367v01n03_04

Meyer, E. J., Regan, P. V., & Jenkins, K. (2022). Transgender at school: Teaching, learning, and socialization. In M. I. Suárez & M. M. Mangin (Eds), *Trans studies in K-12 education: Creating an agenda for research and practice*. Harvard Education Press.

Miller, sj. (2019a). *About gender identity justice in schools and communities*. Teachers College Press.

Miller, sj. (2019b). *Teaching, affirming, and recognizing trans* and gender creative youth: A queer literacy framework*. Palgrave Macmillan UK.

Muhammad, G. E. (2018). A plea for identity and criticality: Reframing literacy learning standards through a four-layered equity model. *Journal of Adolescent & Adult Literacy, 62*(2), 137–142.

Muhammad, G. (2020). *Cultivating genius: An equity framework for culturally and historically responsive literacy*. Scholastic Incorporated.

Muhammad, G. E., & Mosley, L. T. (2021). Why we need identity and equity learning in literacy practices: Moving research, practice, and policy forward. *Language Arts, 98*(4), 189–196.

NASA.gov. (2023). "What is the 5E instructional Model?" https://nasaeclips.arc.nasa.gov/teachertoolbox/the5e

Stryker, S. (2017). *Transgender history: The roots of today's revolution.* Hachette UK.

Suárez, M. I., & Mangin, M. M (Eds.) (2022). *Trans studies in K-12 education: Creating an agenda for research and practice.* Harvard Education Press.

Suárez, M. I., Meister, S. M., & Lindner, A. L. (2019) Envisioning queer curricula: A systematic review of LGBTIQ+ topics in teacher practitioner literature. *Journal of LGBT Youth, 18*:3, 239–255. https://doi.org/10.1080/19361653.2019.1705223

The Queer Mathematics Teacher. (2023). https://www.thequeermathematicsteacher.com/

Younes, S. N. (2018, December). *A short history of trans people's long fight for equality* [Video]. TED Conferences. https://www.ted.com/talks/samy_nour_younes_a_short_history_of_trans_people_s_long_fight_for_equality

Zaino, K. (2021). Queer worldmaking. In *Encyclopedia of queer studies in education* (pp. 578–582). Brill.

PART ONE

Affirming Selfhood

In this section, lessons and vignettes explore selfhood, and affirming and supporting identities.

> *"I'm one of those people who, from earliest memory, always felt feminine-identified even though I was assigned male at birth, even though everybody considered me to be a boy and raised me as such, and even though my body was apparently a typical male body. I didn't have any good explanation for those feelings when I was younger, and after a lifetime of reflection and study I'm still open-minded about how best to explain them. Not that I feel the need to explain them in order to justify my existence. I know only that those feelings persist no matter what. I know that they make me who I am to myself, whatever other people may feel about me or do toward me for having them."*
>
> — Susan Stryker[1]

---

1. Stryker, S. (2017). *Transgender history: The roots of today's revolution.* Hachette UK. p. x.

TRANSformational LOTUS: A HAIKU

Life is muddy
Lotus Flowers grow here
Waves bring self-love

— Bobbi Evans-Santiago

CHAPTER ONE

Exploring and Reclaiming Home in Our Bodies

K. ELLIOTT

Introduction

THESE LESSONS ARE INSPIRED by my personal gender journey, as well as my learnings from trans* and gender-expansive youth who have shared their brilliant audacity for thriving. Through individual and collective reflection, storytelling, movement, and artistic expression, these activities provide space for youth to explore the concept of "home" across multiple dimensions.

I've learned that finding a place of home in our bodies is critical to our well-being as trans* people. Through a practice of movement and embodiment, taking time to just BE in my body without the need for performance or protection has been healing. I've also seen the power of art, writing, and storytelling, through my work with young people, as an opportunity to reclaim our narratives and to see the expansiveness of our lives and communities. Versions of these activities have been facilitated with youth in school-based, community-based, and residential program settings in isolation or as a series of 1- to 2-hour sessions. They evolved over time based on youth feedback and experiences in practice. For this book, I was inspired to pull these ideas together in a way that could be used within a longer youth (or multigenerational) retreat.

Note: I have found that group agreements/norms and a baseline level of trust is needed among participants and with the facilitator before beginning these activities.

"What comes to mind when I imagine affirming trans* and gender creative communities is having folks show up and care about our narratives because we exist. We have the

> *chance to educate others, to say, 'Hey, this is who I am. And what I represent, we actually have a lot more in common than we think.' By opening that space up, trans* folks can feel affirmed, and other people can reflect and say, 'This person isn't really what I thought, either culturally or in society.' [There] are dangerous stereotypes that exist, and I think having that space to really listen can shift people's perspectives. By accepting and collaborating more openly and freely there can be a real shift in our society."* – B. Flores

Details

Topics/Curricular Connections

- Social and Emotional Learning
- Creative Arts (visual art and music)
- Writing
- Culture and History

Grade Level/Audience

- Grade 9 and up

Learning Objectives

Students/participants will come to know and/or be able to do the following:

- Through music, movement, and mindfulness, participants will reflect on joy, relief, and a feeling of being at home in their physical body.
- Participants will utilize storytelling to understand and empathize with the experiences of others in relation to their body, and find connections across identities, cultures, and life experiences.

Common Core Standards

- SL 9-10.1 Initiate and participate effectively in a range of collaborative discussions
- SL 11-12 Present information, findings, and supporting evidence
- ADV.DA.Cr1 Synthesize content generated from stimulus material. Experiment and take risks to discover a personal voice to communicate artistic intent.

Materials

- Comfortable space for sitting, breathing, and movement
- Writing and drawing paper
- Writing and drawing utensils (colorful pens, markers, etc.)
- Something to play music and videos on (and perhaps speakers)
- Whiteboard and markers or equivalent

EXPLORING AND RECLAIMING HOME IN OUR BODIES

Compelling Questions

- In what ways can we create a holistic, thriving home in our bodies?

Lesson Duration

- One-half to one full day

Pedagogical Notes

- The facilitator models introducing themselves and their multiple identities, values, and history to create space for authentic sharing amongst participants.
- Community building is consent-based, and individuals can share about themselves to the degree they are comfortable. The activities provide a multitude of avenues for individual and group participation.
- The facilitator is a participant, fully engaging in the creative expression, mindfulness, storytelling, and reflection elements of the activities.
- The facilitator utilizes multi-sensory approaches (energetic music; guided meditation and body connection; simple visual and verbal instructions; individualized reading and writing; and group discussion).
- Accessibility modifications may be used, including alt text, transcription/CC, and adaptive movement.
- Ample time is allotted for community building, music and movement, and artistic expression, and these activities are not scored, removing the pressures of time and high performance.
- Group work is scaffolded so that participants know how to engage with one another once they are in groups and how to engage with the larger group once they return.

> *"As an educator, I think, for me, that's really about putting systems in place to make sure that kids' identities are respected and supported every time. Not just in one classroom of the one person at their school who's supportive. I think that affirmation can look like other things, it can look like unconditional positive regard, and it doesn't very often look that way. I don't think that's an experience we have much, but I wish we had [it] more. I think it's also about moving from . . . heroes and holidays . . . towards allowing spaces to be trans*-centered."* – M. Rice

Lesson Steps

Engaging Students

- Inform participants that they will be doing activities to deepen their understanding of their body as a space of "home."

- Activate prior knowledge and beliefs about the concept of "home" through storytelling:
  - Encourage participants to honor and listen deeply to the stories of others.
  - Radical Vision Writing/Drawing and Sharing:
    - <u>Individual</u>: Invite participants to imagine and write or draw their vision of "home." (15 min.)
      Ask (and post for reflection as everyone is writing):
      - ☐ What is your vision of the "home" you want for yourself?
      - ☐ What does that "home" look, feel, taste, sound, smell like?
      - ☐ What elements (people, objects, places, activities, etc.) represent home to you?
      - ☐ What are some unique aspects of who you are, or want to be that are reflected in the home you've imagined?
    - <u>Group</u>: Share out (15 min.): While participants share what they came up with, ask for two volunteers to capture key words or phrases on flip chart paper or a whiteboard.
  - Watch the video listed below to learn a bit about the House and Ballroom community, including chosen family and responses to being unhoused, to help participants imagine a radical idea of "home."
    - Michael Roberson on the Ballroom Freedom School (13 min)
    - Reflect on the following questions (10 min):
      - ☐ What are some societal expectations facing house and ballroom youth, and specifically related to their bodies, that interrupt their joy?
      - ☐ How can societal expectations about beauty—and the dynamics of race, gender expression, body shape, and body size—influence our sense of peace and home in our bodies?
      - ☐ What are ways we can envision or reclaim our bodies as "home"?
  - After everyone who wants to speak has shared, review the key words and phrases previously captured on flip chart paper or whiteboard to see if participants want to add anything. Reflect as a group on common themes, observations, connections, and ideas that resonate (5 min).
  - Starting with the list generated, work as a group to create a shared definition of "home" that encompasses the multiple dimensions, cultures, experiences, and visions of those in the space (15 min).

Exploring Concepts, Skills, and Experiences

- Settling into the body: Body Scan (10–12 min)
  - Facilitator should use a slow steady pace and calming tone of voice for this exercise, pausing between each question and instruction.
  - (Optional) Facilitator may choose to play soft instrumental music in the background.

EXPLORING AND RECLAIMING HOME IN OUR BODIES

- Alternatively, facilitators can use an audio recording by Ray Lewey, Vanessa Marrufo, or Alli Simon, or follow this 15-Minute Mindfulness Body Scan script.
- Let participants know that the group will explore ways they can feel at home in their bodies. We will begin by using a body scan exercise to bring mindfulness to physical bodies.
- Invite participants to spread out so they have enough personal space to sit or lie down in comfort.
- Ask participants to find a comfortable body position, putting their feet flat on the floor or lying on the floor (adapt as needed for accessibility).
- Once settled, ask participants to close their eyes for silent reflection.
- Say: "Begin to notice your breath, in and out." (Pause 2–3 seconds between each statement)
  - Notice as your breath enters your nostrils, travels down to your lungs, and causes your belly to expand. Notice as you breathe out your belly contracts and air moves up through the lungs back up through the nostrils or mouth.
  - Invite your full attention to flow in and out with your breath, letting other thoughts drift away.
  - Simply observe your breath and accept it without judgment. There is no need to change anything.
  - Our breath is always there for us. . . . a place of home we can return to at any time.
- "Ask yourself" (Pause 3–5 seconds between each question):
  - How am I feeling in my body?
  - Where is it warm or cool?
  - Where is it centered and still?
  - Where does it want to move?
  - Where is there tightness?
  - How am I breathing?
- Say (pause 3–5 seconds between each statement):
  - As you breathe, begin to notice your head.
  - Notice the muscles in your face and jaw.
  - Notice your neck and shoulders. Is there anything you are holding?
  - Notice your arms. . . . and down to your hands and fingers.
  - Bring awareness to your hips, and however they are resting in this moment.
  - Notice your legs, your ankles, down to your toes and to the bottoms of your feet.
  - Bring your attention back to your heartspace, and to your lungs as you breathe in and out.

- Feel the warm glow of wholeness spreading from your heart throughout the rest of your body.
- Accept whatever comes up here, and let it be. . . . focusing our attention on our joy and wholeness.
- Put one hand over your heart. Just rest it there as you breathe.
- Begin to notice your belly, your core, your center. Rest your other hand on your belly, just below your belly button.
- Feel your breath go in through your nostrils, into your lungs, and all the way down to your belly. Then up from your belly through your lungs and out through your mouth.
  - Let's all take a few slow deep breaths together using a technique called box breathing. (You can also use this video by Conscious Works as a visual prompt for participants.)
    - Breathe in (Count 1,2,3,4), hold (Count 1,2,3,4), out (Count 1,2,3,4), hold (Count 1,2,3,4)
    - Repeat 2–3 more times.
  - If your eyes are closed, you can slowly open them. Notice how you feel.
- Quick write (3 min.):
  - Share one place or situation in which you feel comfortable, at ease, or "home."
  - What do you see/hear/smell/taste/feel in that place or situation?
  - You know how you can feel your atmosphere? Like when there's the thick, heavy air of tension between people or in an environment? Or when you feel loved, and the air feels warm and buoyant? When you imagine feeling comfortable, at ease, or "home," what is that atmosphere like?"
  - **Invite participants to stay connected to that place and to their bodies. Let them know you're moving into a free movement and music activity.
- Music and Movement (10–15 min)
  - Note that participants can move in whatever way brings them a sense of freedom, pleasure, and liberation of body and spirit—dancing, stretching, shaking, and so on.
  - Play music and create open space for dance or movement of any type. Emphasize and encourage exploration of bodies as a place of home. Celebrate any and all bodies and types of movement!

Explaining Observations and Findings

- Use a routine like Think Pair Share and ask participants:
  - How did you feel before we began the body scan and free movement?
  - How do you feel now, afterwards?
  - What did you notice in your body as you moved through the activities?

- What thoughts came up for you?
- What comes to mind when you think about the idea of "feeling at home in your body?"
- Does your earlier thinking about "home" change when you shift focus this way? How?

Elaborating on Learning

- As a group, update the collective definition of "home" to include participants' new reflections.
  - Facilitators can listen for and bring attention to discussion about how societal values/expectations of beauty—and the dynamics of race, gender expression, shape/size, etc. influence people's sense of peace and home in their bodies.
  - Facilitators can listen for and bring attention to discussion about signals bodies give when people's "home" is out of balance or stressed. They might invite conversation about how to nurture, protect, and support one's body.

> *"I think it's when the physical changes start because we've talked about hormones and that's a big deal. If you start later, it's puberty all over again and that's hell. But I think the real deal is the surgery because that is a hands-on experience, and you need somebody else. Some people have partners, and that's great. But 9 times out of 10, you have to have a sibling or parent, and I had surgery, and I didn't have that same support. And I had complications, I had my stitches pop open. And I had to get them closed before college started. Anything can happen, any complications of anything. When my stitches popped open my mom was like, 'Well, you wanted it' and I'm like, 'I didn't want a hole in my side where I can see my organs, I didn't want that, I just wanted to not have a chest anymore and that was it.' But it's more so just help in any way that you can, if you know we're having a surgery and we're gonna struggle a little bit, we can't do basic human needs, offer to help."* – D. Hughes

Evaluating Learning

- Use an exit ticket or similar quick tool to ask participants:
  - What did you learn today?
  - How do you imagine using that learning in your life?
  - What would have made this experience better for you?

Possible Lesson Extensions

Facilitators can build additional explorations of "home" through the lens of the spaces where people spend their daily lives and sleep (houses, shelters, streets, etc.), as well as their larger communities. For example, facilitators might:

- Explore the ways that home is defined across cultures and throughout history.
- Share texts underscoring gender-expansive identities and expressions, and gender roles within homes.
- Share examples of mutual aid and grassroots housing models focused on ensuring all people have a home and specifically uplift examples and spaces led by and for transgender and gender-expansive people, and particularly BIPOC T*GC people supporting one another. Examples include: Trans Housing Coalition, House of Tulip, My Sistah's House.
- Invite participants to research, identify, and share (photos, short video, or writing) examples of mutual aid and collective care in their local community. This can be formal (i.e., organizations, faith groups, house and ballroom community, etc.) or informal (i.e., neighbors caring for one another's children, free libraries/pantries).
- Ask participants to grapple with questions like:
  - How has American individualism driven our current constructs of home?
  - How have historical and current forced displacement, migration, segregation, housing discrimination, etc., influenced our collective understanding of home?
  - In what ways do individuals and families create spaces of home and of thriving, even through challenges?
  - Resources include: Systemic Inequality: Displacement, Exclusion, Segregation, Civil Rights in America: Racial Discrimination in Housing, NCTE - Housing and Homelessness.
- Engage in a deeper study of history and vision of House and Ballroom communities through video and article review and discussion:
  - The Cost of Identity: Twiggy Garçon on LGBTQ+ youth homelessness, house-ballroom, and working on 'Pose'
  - From Pain Comes Strength: Families, Ballroom, and Resistance
  - In Boston, ballroom culture offers freedom for queer and trans* POC
  - Ballroom Freedom School

> "Almost all of my teachers were white growing up. When they looked at me, they saw yet another Brown kid in their classroom, so they never checked in about anything. Simply humanizing other people that didn't look like them would have been nice. Now, as an adult, I can acknowledge why I was going through what I was going through and reacting the way that I was. Checking in to see how students are doing can be so easy, and it's what I needed growing up: simply asking how someone is doing, what you can do to help, asking what they need can change someone's day as well as their future." – B. Flores

Applying the Three Guiding Frameworks

This music, movement, and mindfulness lesson specifically explores and affirms body positivity. It is also responsive to T*GC young peoples' needs and desires to develop celebratory relationships with our bodies. One of the warm-up activities centers the strengths, experiences, and needs of Black T*GC communities and celebrates mutual aid, solidarity, and collective care in these communities.

The Gender Identity Complexities Framework

This lesson offers an opportunity to center *gender complexity* from the start by asking facilitators to model introductions with their name, pronouns, and other relevant social identities (e.g., race, gender identity/expression, sexual orientation, disability, and so on). Participants are then invited to introduce themselves in the same way. Between this opening ritual and the opportunities to imagine, write, draw, and speak aloud throughout the lesson, participants are invited to *self-define*, sharing their personal identities, values, and vision.

Throughout the lesson, participants are asked to *think critically* about societal expectations about bodies—from race to gender expression, body shape, and body size—that interrupt joy and undermine people's ability to feel at peace and at home in their bodies. This inquiry is grounded in developing *critical awareness* of factors, including rejection, that get in the way of safety and stable housing for Black and Latiné LGBTQ+/SGL youth and adults.

Finally, the music and movement component of the lesson invites bold, *authentic* expressions of gender and body positivity, while mindfulness invites quiet reflection on the ways we inhabit our physical selves.

The Bridge to Thriving Framework

Throughout the lesson, participants celebrate their own *identity and selfhood* and build *community* through storytelling, artistic expression, and cultivating shared language. Participants will explore their values, cultures, and the complexities of their intersectional identities as they "locate" themselves within multiple dimensions of home and explore what that means for Thriving.

Through writing, storytelling, and artistic expression participants will engage in *abundance* thinking and futuristic visioning. Creative expression offers an opportunity to visualize wholeness as a healthy escape from stressors. These activities also provide opportunities to recognize pleasure and *relief* in our bodies, physical spaces, communities, and more.

Additionally, the body scan is an invitation to pause and *simply be*—truly finding a sense of home and relief in our physical bodies. The structure of all of the lessons is intended to provide space for relaxation—without the pressures of time, grades, or competition.

The Historically Responsive Literacy Framework

Storytelling activities engage participants to reflect on their values, cultures, *multiple identities*, experiences, and selfhood to conceptualize "home." Participants engage in community building and gain a deeper understanding of the experiences of their peers through listening to one another's stories and creating collective meaning of the word "home."

Through reading selected texts, reflection writing, discussion, and artistic expression, participants build *intellect* and increase *skillfulness* in critical thinking, communication, and articulating their vision of home and thriving* in unique ways. *Criticality* will be used to analyze the historical and current conditions and systems that create barriers to Thriving*, particularly for Black, Indigenous, and Latiné LGBTQ+/SGL youth. Participants will also practice recognizing and uplifting strengths, resources, and examples of Thriving* within House and Ballroom communities.

Finally, music, movement, and mindfulness will be used to explore participant embodiment of *joy* and feeling of home in their physical body. Joy and pleasure will also be cultivated through community building and authentic connections with peers.

References

Adidas Women. (2019, April 22). *9 min guided body scan meditation with Alli Simon* [Video]. YouTube. https://www.youtube.com/watch?v=5qHC1-KCgIM

ArtsEverywhere. (n.d.). *Ballroom Freedom School.* https://www.artseverywhere.ca/series/ballroom-freedom-school/

ArtsEverywhere. (2016, September 10). *Michael Roberson on the Ballroom Freedom School* [Video]. Vimeo. vimeo.com/216007645

Center for American Progress. (2019, August 7). *Systemic inequality: Displacement, exclusion, and segregation – How America's housing system undermines wealth building in communities of color.* https://www.americanprogress.org/article/systemic-inequality-displacement-exclusion-segregation/

Conscious Works. (2020, July 13). *Box breathing: 1 minute in length.* YouTube. https://www.youtube.com/watch?v=n6RbW2LtdFs

Gray, A. (2022, February 24). In Boston, ballroom culture offers freedom for queer and trans POC. *Boston University Radio.* https://www.wbur.org/news/2022/02/24/boston-ballroom-culture-freedom-queer-trans-poc

Headspace. (2022, June 29). *Learn breathing technique box breathing: Practice breathwork for focus and anxiety with Dora Kamau.* YouTube. https://www.youtube.com/watch?v=a7uQXDkxEtM

House of Tulip. (n.d.) *Home.* https://houseoftulip.org/

Jackson, J. (2019, July 10). From pain comes strength: Families, ballroom, and resistance. An interview with Fatha Jazz Bordeaux. *Walker Reader.* https://walkerart.org/magazine/fatha-jazz-bordeaux-twin-cities-ballroom

Lassiter, M. D., & Salvatore, S. C. (2021). Civil rights in America: Racial discrimination in housing. *The National Historic Landmarks Program, National Park Service.* https://www.nps.gov/subjects/nationalhistoriclandmarks/upload/Civil_Rights_Housing_NHL_Theme_Study_revisedfinal.pdf

Lewey, R. (2021). *Trans embodiment: Coming home to ourselves* [Video]. Insight Timer https://insighttimer.com/raylewey/guided-meditations/trans-embodiment-coming-home-to-ourselves

Main, P. (2022, October 21). *Exit tickets*. https://www.structural-learning.com/post/exit-tickets

Policy Research Associates. (2022, January 13). *Mindfulness exercise: Body scan* [Video]. YouTube. https://www.youtube.com/watch?v=e0f9wa2SUX0

Mindful Schools. (n.d.). *15-minute mindfulness body scan script for teens*. https://drive.google.com/file/d/1iKY05ReW0ru5qvxVG1vVmWNxrljRs0Bv/view?usp=drive_link

My Sistah's House. (n.d.). *Home*. https://mshmemphis.org/

National Center for Transgender Equality. (n.d.) *Issues: Housing & homelessness*. https://transequality.org/issues/housing-homelessness

Public Broadcasting Service. (2020, February 10). The cost of identity: Twiggy Garçon on LGBTQ+ youth homelessness, house-ballroom, and working on 'Pose' [Web series episode]. In *Chasing the Dream*. https://www.pbs.org/wnet/chasing-the-dream/2020/02/twiggy-garcon-on-lgbtq-youth-homelessness/

Teach For Life. (2018, September 20). *Think pair share*. YouTube. https://www.youtube.com/watch?v=Mig4olzUy4M

Trans Housing Coalition. (n.d.). *Home*. https://www.transhousingcoalition.org/

CHAPTER TWO

Brain Chemicals and Kindness

BRE EVANS-SANTIAGO

Introduction

WITH DEPRESSION BEING SUCH a concern among T*GC folx, and mental health in crisis nationwide, it is important for children to learn early on that they have the power to trigger brain chemicals to increase happiness. The bans across the country against mentioning diverse people (i.e., banning Black history, LGBTQ+ recognition, drag story hours, etc.), are silencing, devastating to mental health, and can make it difficult to feel proud. Building "happy" brain circuitry early on establishes a powerful foundation for lifelong well-being and can be augmented through events and actions that will be ingrained within the brain moving forward.

In this lesson, children dance/move, sing, and read as ways to increase their "happy" brain chemicals. They learn what happy chemicals are and what humans can do to activate them. The simple act of giving a high five, for example, or playing with someone on the playground can increase oxytocin and serotonin levels.

To develop math and science skills, students map happiness events on a bar graph, analyzing results such as, "Largest number of . . . ," "The difference between . . . ," "Mean, median, mode," and the ways that data varies by actions, their impact, and change over time. They will also fill up a wall-mounted image of a bucket with stickers to represent their "emotional buckets" being filled when someone or something made them feel good.

> *"I've done training for educators or for in and after-school professionals. It is really kind of my jam. And I hear from a lot of people who say, I am 100% here for this, but my organization is not there yet. That doesn't matter. Right. I think that's what I want people to know, the school that I went to in middle school is still not there. They still are not accepting or affirming or even supportive of trans* kids. But all it took was that one*

> *teacher for me, that's all that it takes. Statistically, we have data to show us that it takes one caring adult to actually affirm a young person's identity to cut their suicidality in half. So, I think that's probably my biggest takeaway for folks is to think like if you are in a system, that's not working, and even if you don't feel like you have the power to change that system, you can look outside the system for us. I can just see the individual, and you absolutely have the power to do something there."* – B. Matthews

Details

Topics/Curricular Connections

- Life Science (and neurochemistry) - Brain chemicals
- Social Emotional Learning
- Healthy human development (survival depends on having one's holistic needs met)

Grade Level/Audience

- Grade 2 and up

Learning Objectives

Students/participants will come to know and/or be able to do the following:

- Compare/contrast oxytocin and serotonin
- Identify events within a text that could increase oxytocin and serotonin
- Set goals for themselves to increase their peers' and their own "happy" brain chemicals
- Students are successful when they can discuss the differences between the two brain chemicals and what can be done to increase them

Common Core Standards

- LS.4.D: Biodiversity and Human Populations live in a variety of habitats, and change in those habitats affects the organisms living there.
- RL.3.3: Describe characters in a story (e.g., their traits, motivations, or feelings) and explain how their actions contribute to the sequence of events.
- RL.4.3: Describe in depth a character, setting, or event in a story or drama, drawing on specific details in the text (e.g., a character's thoughts, words, or actions).
- 3.MD.B.3 Draw a scaled picture graph and a scaled bar graph to represent a data set with several categories. Solve one- and two-step "how many more" and "how many less" problems using information presented in scaled bar graphs.
- Science (general): Constructing Explanations and Designing Solutions Constructing explanations and designing solutions in grades 3–5 builds on K–2

experiences and progresses to the use of evidence in constructing explanations that specify variables that describe and predict phenomena and in designing multiple solutions to design problems. Use evidence (e.g., observations, patterns) to construct an explanation.

Materials

- The book *Julián Is a Mermaid* by Jessica Love
- The "Happy" music video by Pharrell Williams
- Interactive kindness graph
- Large bucket image for wall
- Stickers (colored dots are easiest for this project)
- Teacher-created slides with definitions and discussion prompts

Compelling Questions

- What does our brain need to make us feel happy?
- What could we do for ourselves or others to increase our happy brain chemicals?

Supporting Questions

- Why do we not feel happy all the time?
- What could our class do to increase happy brain chemicals?
- What actions might help us and others to feel happiness?

Lesson Duration

This lesson is likely to take about 2 hours, but it can extend much longer. Students can keep collecting data on their graph or in the bucket and be in continuous conversation about actions that promote happiness, as well as their impact.

Pedagogical Notes

- In preparation for activities that come after reading *Julián Is a Mermaid*, create a large image of a bucket that can be attached to the wall.
- You will also need an x-y-axis chart to create a bar graph. This can be created on large poster paper or purchased pre-drawn, and there should be circle stickers or a way to color in bars quickly throughout the week when someone has performed a kind action. The graph should have space to list actions that can create happiness on the x-axis and numbers counting by 1s on the y-axis. Pre-fill a few general kind acts that the class will use as a whole and leave room for students to add a few more.
- See examples of the bucket and graph in our online resource repository.
- This lesson can be taught to older students using either the same or other texts and including all four "happy" brain chemicals dopamine, oxytocin, serotonin, and endorphins (DOSE).

Lesson Steps

Engaging Students

- Begin the lesson by playing the song "Happy" by Pharrell Williams to catch students' attention. Encourage dancing, movement, and/or singing along.
- After the song, ask
    - "When you hear music, how does it affect you?"
    - "Are there songs that make you happy? Sad? Other feelings?"
    - "What about those songs makes you feel those feelings?"
- Inform the students that today they will learn about what can help people to feel happy.

> *"When I think of affirmation, I think of supportive friends. When I came out to my friends, . . . it really helped in a lot of ways for [them] to say, 'If you ever need something, or someone to talk to, I'm there for you.' This makes you feel seen. To have someone to rely on, or to be able to talk to, or to feel open with is supportive. Affirming is being there for somebody.*
>
> *Affirmation is also about belonging at school. At my school, we have books in our library that have a rainbow sticker on the spine. Those are the books that have LGBTQIA+ representation and it's just amazing to see yourself represented in little areas, or little things like a rainbow banner, it's those little things that help you feel seen and safe and that is what affirming is and what I hope to see in every single school."* – E. Chen

Exploring Concepts, Skills, and Experiences

Define

Use slides or another format to display definitions of "happy brain chemicals"[1]:

- Happy brain chemicals are triggered, and new circuits are built, when we feel accepted, loved, and useful.
- Serotonin circuits are built with friendships, respect, love, and trust.
- Happy brain chemicals are also triggered, and new circuits are built, when we do nice things for others because it makes us feel good inside.
- Oxytocin circuits are built with love and kind touch (hugs, high fives).

Discuss

- When we experience something that causes our body to release oxytocin or serotonin, "the chemicals tell our brain that what just happened was good, so then we like it, and want to keep doing [that thing]."
- "We don't always have happy feelings and that's okay. Sometimes we need to feel sad or cry. Sometimes we feel angry when something feels unfair. No feeling

lasts forever - we feel feelings, and then they pass, and later they come back, and pass again. What else can make us *not* happy?"

Assess

- On a piece of chart paper or other medium, capture students' answers to the following questions. You will use them later for the classroom graph.
  - What is something that you have done for others that made you feel good?
  - What is something that someone has done for you that made you feel good?

Explaining Observations and Findings

Reflecting on the class' listed experiences, inform them that they will read a story together titled, *Julián Is a Mermaid*. Here is a link to the read-aloud of the book.

Ask the following questions (or revise to your liking) while reading aloud:

- When Julián and his abuela are on the train, Julián sees something that triggers happiness. What does he see? Why do you think it makes him happy?
- The next few pages are Julián experiencing something. What is he experiencing? Could he create happy chemicals alone? Explain.
- When Julián is alone and uses his imagination, he transforms. What does he transform into? How does his abuela respond? What do you think is happening with Julián's brain chemicals as he imagines and as his abuela responds?
- When Julián walks down the street dressed as a mermaid, he could feel many different ways. What are some examples of how Julián could feel? From the pictures and words, how do you think he actually feels? What do you think helps him feel that way? We know that certain kinds of experiences can build serotonin brain circuits or oxytocin brain circuits—let's refer back to our slide. What "happy" brain circuits could be building for Julián? Explain.
- Let's describe what happens when Julián joins the parade. What actions occur there and how might he and others feel? How might serotonin or oxytocin be building circuits in his brain?

Elaborating on Learning

Make sure that your graphing chart and bucket are displayed before continuing with the lesson:

- You can say something like, "Now as a class, we are going to investigate creating happiness at school. This week, we will engage in acts of kindness as a class, and you can also do some on your own. When you perform a kind act, come in and put a green sticker in the graph column that matches your action. [Teachers are encouraged to provide an example, so students see how this works.] If being kind also made you feel good, take a red sticker and put it inside the bucket on

the wall. If someone did something for you that made you happy, also put a sticker in the bucket."
- As a formative assessment, you can note how students engage with the bucket and graph, with attention to how they talk about this activity with their peers.
- At the end of the week, compare how many actions were taken, as shown on the graph, to how much the class's "feel good" bucket is filled.

Evaluating Learning

At the end of the week, revisit the slides and conversation about kindness and happy brain chemicals to prepare for a summative assessment:

- The students will share one action that they took, which chemical was probably increased, and why. Sharing could be in the form of a video such as Flipgrid, written out, or illustrated with an explanation, for example a comic strip. Offering options provides an opportunity for self-expression, which is a Universal Design for Learning (UDL) practice.
- Once the students create their pieces, they may share them with the teacher or in small groups with peers.

Note: This activity does not have to end! Keep the chart and bucket up on the wall and add to them throughout the year. They can always be revisited when the time is right.

> *"My dream for our community as trans* and gender creative folks would be affirming the full spectrum of transness and all of the beauty and creativity, and fullness and richness and life that we bring. And so, affirmation to me within the community would just be making space for all of us. Trans* community is not pie, there is enough for all of us. There are spaces and pockets for all of us to be our full, beautiful authentic selves, without judging the way a person presents or if they take hormones or don't, or if they have surgery. I don't think anybody, cis or trans* or queer, is stagnant. Our identities are always changing. [We need to leave] space for that growth to continue to happen."* – B. Kennedy

Applying the Three Guiding Frameworks

The choice to read *Julián Is a Mermaid* is responsive to gender creative students' need to see themselves represented in the curriculum. It also provides a broader opportunity for exposure, discussion, and inquiry as it relates to Julián being happy while dressing in a gender non-conforming way and being supported by his abuela and others. This encourages being accepting of and kind to people who may be or act differently than what students are accustomed to. Also, as students track their positive experiences and acts of kindness, they are given the space to affirm people for who they are.

The Gender Identity Complexities Framework

Gender complexities are addressed with the text, *Julián Is a Mermaid*. We use this text to help students think critically about where happiness might come from and how celebrating someone who may seem unique or different from them is just as important as celebrating themselves. When the text is shared, the students see Julián dress as a mermaid. This text helps advocate for gender complexity because society mostly shows mermaids as women. Julián is dressed with long hair and jewelry from their grandmother, demonstrating gender fluidity. The book also provides the space for the students to identify why Julián was happy and what is needed to help Julián's happiness (*authenticity*). This provides an opportunity for discussion about other people they may know who defy societal gender norms. Lastly, *critical consciousness* is addressed in this lesson because the students are able to see gender challenged in the book *Julián Is a Mermaid*. The students are able to see Julián is happily dressed as a mermaid and that people love them and support them. Julián's abuela demonstrates love in a profound way and the students are able to see that when gender is pushed beyond societal expectations.

The Bridge to Thriving Framework

When thinking about the components of the lesson where students are increasing brain chemicals, the petals of the thriving model are addressed. The students will feel *relief* when they practice being kind to one another. It will give students a sense of safety or well-being with acts of kindness. *Pleasure* is addressed when the students show love to one another with encouragement or play together. The students will experience *abundance* by elevating kindness, which expands their knowledge of what it means and how it feels to be kind. When the students show acts of kindness, they will experience internal feelings of satisfaction or happiness as well. This learning of and knowing oneself connects with *selfhood* as confidence builds. Lastly, as the students begin to think about others and how to increase oxytocin and serotonin, they will critically think about who people are and what they need in order to feel happy, which demonstrates the last petal, *community*. Overall, the lesson amplifies how *simply being* yourself and accepted by others produces happiness.

The Historically Responsive Literacy Framework

As the students decide upon acts of kindness, they will work through various components of responsiveness as well. The first concept of *identity* is addressed because the lesson will give students the opportunity to think about others and what people need to increase serotonin and oxytocin. *Literacy skills* are increased when students create their pieces to share what they learned about oxytocin and serotonin (video, slideshow, comic strip, etc.). *Math skills* are used when the students add to their class graph as they do acts of kindness throughout the week. *Science skills* are increased as students learn about two of the four chemicals that build upon happiness within the brain. *Intellect* is developed when the students increase their knowledge about how the brain works when responding to our actions. When the students begin to complete acts of kindness throughout the week, they will have to pay attention to others and their needs. They should notice assets and marginalizations within their schools/communities, which will increase *criticality* as they strive to build happy chemicals. Lastly, *joy* is addressed when the students bring smiles in and out of the classroom while setting goals for acts of kindness. They will also see their graph increase when they take more action, and that will correlate with pride and self-satisfaction.

Note

1. Breuning, 2016

References

Breuning, L. G. (2016). *Habits of a happy brain: Retrain your brain to boost your serotonin, dopamine, oxytocin, and endorphin levels*. Adams Media.

Evans-Santiago, B. (2023). *Bucket example*. https://drive.google.com/file/d/1r4NFL9FuyLbdxI4N-zzIg0AMykULhYJw/view?usp=drive_link

Evans-Santiago, B. (2023). *Kindness graph example*. https://drive.google.com/file/d/1igiGhqA0nrowqzOf699hP5qyCKEYJf22/view?usp=drive_link

Learn Conmigo 123. (2021, January 28). *Julián is a mermaid read aloud* [Video]. YouTube. https://www.youtube.com/watch?v=62HGRe_QuhU

Love, J. (2018). *Julián is a mermaid*. Candlewick Press.

iamOTHER. (2014, January 8). *Pharrell Williams – Happy (official music video)* [Video]. YouTube. https://www.youtube.com/watch?v=y6Sxv-sUYtM

CHAPTER THREE

Who Are You?: A Black Queer Journey to Selfhood and Community

Danelle Adeniji and DeKeisha Smith

Introduction

This lesson is designed to help Black LGBTQ+ and same-gender-loving students critically reflect on their identities and the power of self-definition, as well as understand the significance of creating supportive, inclusive spaces for Black and other LGBTQ+/SGL individuals. We use Sullivan's (2019) definition of queering, which she describes as an embodiment and teaching of self-expression to counter dominant gender, sexuality, and identity narratives for educators in any space they occupy. Furthermore, queer is inclusive of trans* and gender-expansive folks.

Through freedom journaling, research on historical figures, and reading and analyzing a text, students will explore their own identities and the identities of others. Throughout the unit, students will center the experiences and perspectives of Black, Queer, and trans* individuals, and focus on both the importance of resistance to oppressive narratives and the creation of inclusive, supportive spaces.

Audre Lorde (2007) states that we, Black people, must define ourselves for ourselves before white supremacy imposes its own oppressive narrative. Genishi and Dyson (2009) further note that children's lives are mapped out in educational spaces by people who neither share their communities nor actively seek out their voices. Black Queer cultural knowledge is reduced, stripped away, and replaced with Eurocentric ways of knowing, leaving our rich cultural values and backgrounds labeled subordinate. Deficit thinking such as anti-Blackness and cisheteropatriarchy dominate educational spaces, forcing false information onto Black Queer and trans* students in an attempt to tell them who they are, and who it's possible for them to become. This instructional unit is a disruption of that. We hope it will be an engaging and thought-provoking journey for students and teachers alike.

> *"Elementary school was more related to gender performance, because I went to elementary school in an all-Black neighborhood school, but I was with the girls . . . outside making up cheers, and dancing. I was not playing football . . . I was not interested in sports. My dad is a head football coach [and] that was such a thing (and still is today). They definitely did what they could. Specifically, my kindergarten teacher, who I still love to this day, always provided a nice, fun space for me. And when the kids would start being rude, it was helpful. I honestly didn't even know what that word was at that time. I know that I kept being called it. I knew it was a bad word because of the way [kids] were sharing it. But it took me a while, like until fifth grade, to make a correlation between my feminine energy and what they were saying. Anytime my elementary school teachers heard that type of talk, they were very disciplinary: 'That's not a good word.' 'Don't talk to each other that way,' kind of, but in later grades—first, second, third—some of them [would also say], 'But I'm going to call your dad and I'm going to tell him that you are doing this with the girls that you probably shouldn't do because you're a boy.' Those were bad moments. They definitely were like, 'Yeah, he's playing with dolls and not playing with soccer balls. He's dressing up in girls' clothes, and not playing with blocks,' which then had this trickle effect at home. They did the best they could. But now what I'm getting at school, I'm low-key getting it at home, too."* – Benjamin

Details

Topics/Curricular Connections

- Language Arts
- Reading
- Social Studies

Grade Level/Audience

- Grade 9 and up

Learning Objectives

Students will critically reflect on:

- Their identities,
- Their communities,
- Pro-Black, pro-Queer spaces where they can simply exist,
- What is essential for moving beyond surviving to thriving.

WHO ARE YOU?

Common Core Standards

- 8.CC.1: Cite the textual evidence that most strongly supports an analysis of what the text says explicitly as well as inferences drawn from the text.
- 8.CC.2: Cite the textual evidence that most strongly supports an analysis of what the text says explicitly as well as inferences drawn from the text.
- 8.CC.4: Determine the meaning of words and phrases as they are used in a text, including figurative and connotative meanings; analyze the impact of specific word choices on meaning and tone, including analogies or allusions to other texts.
- 8.CC.3a: Engage and orient the reader by establishing a context and point of view and introducing a narrator and/or characters; organize an event.
- 8.CC.7: Conduct short research projects to answer a question (including a self-generated question), drawing on several sources and generating additional related, focused questions.
- 8.CC.10: Write routinely over extended time frames (time for research, reflection, and revision) and shorter time frames (a single sitting or a day or two) for a range of discipline-specific tasks, purposes, and audiences.

Materials

- Freedom Journals
- Tools to complete digital research (see lesson and resources for detail)
- Book: *The Stars and the Blackness Between Them* by Junauda Petrus

Compelling Questions

- How have members of the Black Queer diaspora imagined and enacted freedom through literature, activism, and simply living their lives?
- What are some of the ways that Black Queer community members have resisted oppressive or deficit narratives?
- How have Black Queer folx imagined and designed community spaces where thriving is possible?

Lesson Duration

- Roughly one semester

Pedagogical Notes

- Give students plenty of time to think, work, collaborate, and be in discussion with each other.
- Facilitators are urged to model sharing pronouns, preferred names, and gender identities as part of community forming and throughout teaching this unit.

Lesson Steps

Freedom Journaling

Robin D. G. Kelley (2003) and Bettina Love (2019) describe freedom dreaming as relying on Black imagination and love to tear down oppressive constructs and the "educational survival complex"[1] to co-construct a new world.

Using this framing, freedom journaling offers opportunities for students and practitioners to reflect on power and their intersectional identities, their communities, their freedom dreams, what they are learning about, their musings, and to imagine the futures they desire. Throughout the experience of unpacking their queerness and Blackness, students can use the journal as a central location for continuous reflection and to return to as they navigate this journey.

Each of the activities presented below makes use of freedom journaling.

Identity Mapping

Students will use the Wheel of Power/Privilege to create an identity map that lists their various in/visible identities. This will encourage them to think beyond binary societal constructs (woman/man, queer/straight, etc.) and build a foundational baseline, both for themselves and for the activity that follows.

Facilitators can invite students to draw and color their own wheel in their freedom journal or provide a blown-up image of the pre-existing wheel, on which to map their identities, perhaps by coloring or circling the segments where they land.

Figure 3.1.

Wheel of Power/Privilege Adapted by Sylvia Duckworth. Reprinted with permission.

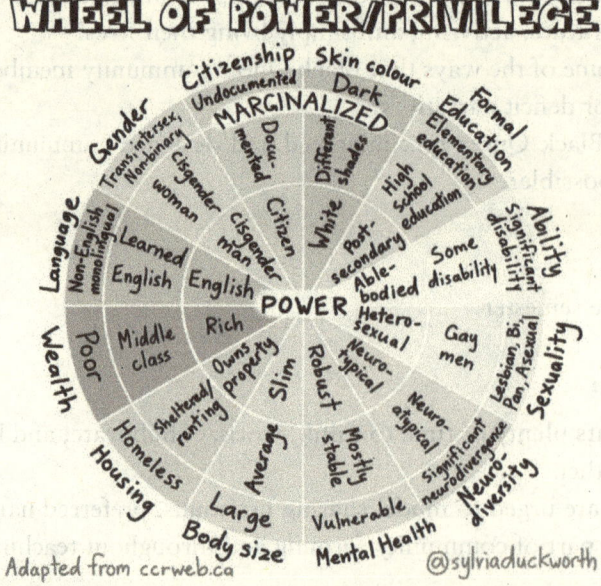

> *"For me, curiosity has always been an important part of responsiveness, as well as gratitude. If a young person tells you something about their identity, it's important to not react with, 'Oh, I knew it. Oh, here's what you need to do next,' or 'Oh, here's what's going to happen next.' It should be 'Hey, I'm grateful that you told me this thing. I'm grateful that I am a part of this moment with you,' and continue with, 'What do you want to do next? What do you think is the best thing to do next?' Especially working with adolescents, they know what they need, or at least they have some sense of what they need on some level. They're usually able to tell us. Or at least tell us what they hope to avoid. What are these young people telling you they need? What does this queer person or person of another marginalized identity need? That autonomy, to say what they need and hopefully then get what they need, is an important part of responsiveness. It seems kind of simple, but it's profound in how simple it is, to be grateful to have a connection with people and curious about how to support them." – M. Luebbert*

Once students have completed their maps, they will break into small groups of three or four students to share and critically analyze what they've noticed. They can be given the thought questions:

- Which of your identity memberships are closest to the center of the wheel and rooted in power, and which are further away?
- Which of your various identity memberships fall on the tier of being historically and intentionally marginalized?
- What are one to two ways that your identity memberships have shaped your lived experience?
- What does queerness look like and mean for you?
- What does Blackness look like and mean for you?

After the discussion, students can journal their thoughts, wonderings, and questions. They might respond to this prompt:

- When I anchor into love for myself and for Black Queer people to imagine a new world, I see/taste/smell/hear/feel. . . .

> *"When I imagine affirming trans* and gender-creative communities, I see a grand pageant, where each person could strut, be introduced as someone beautiful, someone important and special, have their chosen name and pronouns announced to the crowd (so they wouldn't have to do it themselves), and generally bask in the limelight and applause just for the space they take as a human. And yet, I also imagine this pageant to be held in context with cis-people getting the same treatment, so that any trans* and gender-creative people are seen and valued as an equal part of the diverse whole of humanity.*
>
> *For the same reason, I also envision classrooms and meetings and online bios everywhere announcing everyone's pronouns so that no one has to be singled out for needing*

> *to announce them because they may appear counter to people's assumptions and perceptions.*
>
> *And I imagine walking down the street and high-fiving all the trans* and gender-creative people I meet, thanking them for their inspired bravery, for being and staying alive, and just for making it out of the house that day.*
>
> *It's not about singling out, but signaling in."* – K. James

Digging into Identity and Culture

This is a reflective exercise designed to help students think more deeply about their identities and their communities. Invite students to free write in response to the following prompts. You might break this into chunks, with small group discussions spread throughout:

- Write 1–2 sentences that answer the question, "Who are you?"
- We each belong to a number of different communities, whether at school, at programs, or at home. What cultural practices do you and your "at-home community" engage in? (These can be holidays, prayer, eating specific foods, doing regular activities, etc.)
- What ethical beliefs (what's right or wrong, obligations, values, virtues, etc.) does your "at-home community" have? These might be about social issues like gender-affirming spaces or access to healthcare, for example.
    - How do these beliefs show up in your daily life?
- When you think about your community, there's usually an inner circle (people you are closest to, confide in, and trust) and an outer circle (acquaintances, distant relatives, etc.). How would you describe your *inner* circle?
- How much does your *inner* circle mirror your at-home community? (What's similar? What's different?)
- How much does your *outer* circle mirror your at-home community?
- Visioning: This is what I want my community to look/feel/be like . . .
- Now that you've reflected on your communities, take some time to explore your interests. For example, what kinds of artistic representation are you drawn to?
    - What music are you drawn to?
    - What visual art (painting, drawing, etc.) are you drawn to?
    - What media (movies, shows, etc.) are you drawn to?
- How do you like to spend your free time?
- What gives you joy?
- Have you ever experienced a moment when you felt like you could "simply be?" Where you felt whole and at peace? What was that moment like? What might make another moment like that possible?
- At the beginning of this activity, you were asked "Who are you?" How has your answer changed or evolved? Have you noticed anything new about yourself?

Once students have completed their individual reflections, put them into small groups to discuss what an identity-affirming community is like (they could list characteristics, create a character that embodies identity-affirming community, etc.).

Invite the small groups to share their thoughts with the whole class.

Close Reading

Using *The Stars and the Blackness Between Them* (Petrus, 2019) students will unpack, identify, and explore how embracing queerness and Blackness is liberatory and a political act of resistance.[2]

While they are reading the book, invite students to pause, reflect, and journal, particularly after each chapter. Focus on helping them use textual evidence to support their ideas, pulling quotes that offer important information, and noting the page numbers and locations of excerpts or examples.

A guiding question could be: *How is embracing queerness and Blackness used in this text to enact resistance and/or liberation?* Teachers might also consider developing a reading guide with key questions and ideas for each chapter, or using one that already exists online.

In addition to exploring the main themes, conflicts, and characters, you can also revisit the compelling questions and reflections:

- An identity-affirming community includes . . .
- When I anchor into love for myself and for Black Queer people to imagine a new world, I see/taste/smell/hear/feel. . . .
- How have members of the Black Queer diaspora imagined and enacted freedom through literature, activism, and simply living their lives?
- What are some of the ways that Black Queer community members have resisted oppressive or deficit narratives?
- How have Black Queer folx imagined and designed community spaces where thriving is possible?

Teachers can also assign astrological poems from the book for close reading and analysis. See the references at the end of this chapter for astrology resources.

> *"Physical representation is very important to me. I was born and raised in Orange County and attended predominantly white and affluent schools. This is likely why it took me a long time to transition or accept the queer part of myself. I can only recall two queer teachers from my upbringing, and neither of them, as white cisgender men, reflected my gay identity. This is why representation is so powerful. If I were to have had someone that looked like me, I probably would have come out sooner. Cultural representation is equally important when we consider how students of color can feel reinforced or undermined by the adults in front of the room." – B. Flores*

Research - Black LGBTQIA+/SGL Historical Figures

Part One - Historical Figures

In small groups, students will research two Black queer historical figures—Pauli Murray and Marsha P. Johnson—with a focus on how each advanced social support and rights for Black Queer communities. Focus on helping students use textual evidence to support their ideas. This is another place where it could be powerful to revisit the **Compelling Questions**.

In addition to the numerous resources available, digital resources can include:

- The documentary My Name is Pauli Murray
- The video profile, My Name is Pauli Murray: New Film on Black Queer Legal Pioneer Who Inspired RBG & Thurgood Marshall
- The video profile, Activism: Marsha P. Johnson, which is accompanied by teaching materials

Text resources can include:

- The picture book, *Sylvia and Marsha Start a Revolution* by Joy Michael Ellison

Part Two - A Manifesto

> **Content Warning:** The CRC Statement contains mentions of organizing in response to rape and rape crisis.

With revolutionary action, blueprints to freedom, and historical figures in mind, invite students to read the Combahee River Collective Statement.[3] The Statement is presented in four sections, which could be assigned using the jigsaw methodology. Focus on helping them use textual evidence to support their ideas.

As they read this text, students will pay close attention to:

- How the CRC built community;
- The CRC's strategies and tactics for revolutionary action, including:
  - How the CRC called out and responded to oppression/oppressors;
  - How the CRC sought to create oppression-free spaces;
- What the CRC's beliefs were.

Once students have completed their close reading of the CRC Statement, invite them to make connections to the activities that came before: personal identity, community, love, empowerment, activism, and imagining thriving.

They could respond to journal prompts like:

- What does thriving look like and mean for me?
- What do I want my future to look like?

- Who can I co-construct a thriving future with?

Or they can loop back to the **Compelling Questions** or other prompts to elaborate on their thoughts.

For the final project, invite students to use the unit's readings, resources, and activities to design some representation of a thriving future, grounded in identity, community, freedom dreaming, and love.

We recommend inviting students to complete a creative project that represents their unique genius and identities (poetry, manifestos, Pecha Kucha, visual art, lyrics, etc.), which can be presented as a gallery walk. This could be virtual and can be customizable to each student's preferences.

> "I think Pride as celebration is right, but for people who aren't extroverted, it would be more so just kind of that closeness. When you're coming out as—especially being trans* because it's so much different than bisexual or lesbian or gay—this is where you change to become your true self, to show people who you truly are, what you see in the mirror, versus what they see. I think it's more so the closeness of those people who you really want, because this could make or break your life. And you're gonna lose people. I think celebration deals with the people that you want most to understand you, who are gonna accept who you are, and help you become who you are. So, if you're not a person who wants to go out so much, it's a home celebration, talking about how the journey is for you and getting excited and seeing them supporting you and just asking the questions, 'Okay, what can we do?' 'What will this be like?' 'What do you want us to do?' It's having that closeness and that community, whether they're LGBT or not, it's that love and foundation because not a lot of trans* people get that. So, I think that's the celebration of, 'I'm not alone in this.'"– D. Hughes

Applying the Three Guiding Frameworks

The Gender Identity Complexities Framework

With its focus on Queer students, including trans* and gender-creative students, as well as T*GC historical figures and book characters, this unit intentionally addresses and co-constructs an affirming and celebratory *gender complex* space. Black Queer students have the freedom to define themselves for themselves and realize the *expansiveness and fluidity* of queering every space they occupy.

The Bridge to Thriving Framework

This unit offers students, teachers, facilitators, and community members opportunities to explore their *selfhood* critically and deliberately through a focus on identities, *community*, and *simply being*. The unit allows exploration of how queerness and Blackness can be foundational to shaping, understanding, and defining oneself.

The Historically Responsive Literacy Framework

This lesson develops historically responsive literacy through its focus on Black Queer young adult literacy and literature that highlights identities that exist outside of normed traditions and constructions such as gender, sexuality, race, and family. It also highlights Black Queer history and contemporary lived experience.

With regard to HRL's five focal points, this unit offers the following:

- **Identity:** Students unpack and navigate who they are, how queerness shapes their identities and lived experiences, and how their identities shape their freedom dreams.
- **Skills:** Students practice close reading, writing, and critical thinking skills throughout the experience.
- **Intellect:** Through this learning journey, students become "smarter" about critical thinking, Black Queer history, the pathway between surviving and thriving, how powerful ideas are presented through literature and other forms of communication, and where they, with their intersectional in/visible identities, fit into all of this as experts and actors.
- **Criticality:** Students critically reflect on the relationships between identities and power, Black Queer oppression, and possibilities for thriving, and Black Queer activism toward building the spaces they need and deserve.
- **Joy:** Students draw on Queer and Black ideologies to dream and co-construct their futures and a community without oppression.

Notes

1. With the "educational survival complex," Love (2019) advances the observation that rather than being able to thrive, students are forced to be in survival mode as they face the larger society's pervasive inequities and oppressions through the schooling system. This includes punitive, carceral control; competitive, dehumanizing capitalism; cisheteropatriarchy; anti-Blackness; xenophobia; and so on. What should be a rich developmental experience is, instead, a constant barrage of spiritual, and often physical, violence.
2. Adeniji et al., 2022
3. Combahee River Collective, 1977

References

Adeniji, D., Frieson, B., Jiménez-Macias, T., Rasbury, K., Wright, K., & Vickery, A. E. (2022). Exploring Blackness, queerness, and liberation through The Stars and the Blackness Between Them. In *Queer adolescent literature as a complement to the English Language Arts curriculum* (2nd ed.). Rowman & Littlefield.

Alber, R. (2016, December 06). *Enliven class discussions with gallery walks*. Edutopia. https://www.edutopia.org/blog/enliven-class-discussion-with-gallery-walks-rebecca-alber

Astrology.com. (n.d.). *12 zodiac signs: All you need to know*. https://www.astrology.com/zodiac-signs

Combahee River Collective. (1977). *The Combahee River Collective statement*. https://www.blackpast.org/african-american-history/combahee-river-collective-statement-1977/

Cult of Pedagogy. (2015, April 15). *The jigsaw method*. YouTube. https://www.youtube.com/watch?v=euhtXUgBEts

Democracy Now! (2021, January 29). *My name is Pauli Murray: New film on Black queer legal pioneer who inspired RBG & Thurgood Marshall*. YouTube. https://www.youtube.com/watch?v=L3u98p8PDlc

Duckworth, S. (2020, August 19). *Wheel of power/privilege*. Instagram. https://www.instagram.com/p/CEFiUShhpUT/?utm_source=ig_web_button_share_sheet

Ellison, J. M. (2020). *Sylvia and Marsha start a revolution!: The story of the trans women of color who made LGBTQ+ history*. Jessica Kingsley Publishers.

Genishi, C., & Dyson, A. H. (2009). *Children, language, and literacy: Diverse learners in diverse times*. Teachers College Press.

Kelley, R. D. G. (2003). *Freedom dreams: The Black radical imagination*. Beacon Press.

Libra Moon Astrology. (n.d.). *The seasons in astrology*. http://www.libramoonastrology.com/seasons.html

Lorde, A. (2007). *Sister outsider: Essays and speeches* (Reprint edition). Crossing Press.

Love, B. (2019). *We want to do more than survive: Abolitionist teaching and the pursuit of educational freedom*. Beacon Press.

Petrus, J. (2019). *The stars and the Blackness between them*. Penguin Books.

Public Broadcasting Service Learning Media. (2018). *Activism: Marsha P. Johnson* [Video]. https://ca.pbslearningmedia.org/resource/fp18.lgbtq.marsha.p.johnson/activism-marsha-p-johnson/

Sullivan, M. J. (2019, May 31). Black queer feminism. In *Oxford African American studies center*. Oxford University Press. https://doi.org/10.1093/acref/9780195301731.013.78530

West, B., & Cohen, J. (Directors). (2021, September 17). *My name is Pauli Murray*. Amazon Studios. https://www.amazon.com/My-Name-Pauli-Murray/dp/B09DMPMWCP

CHAPTER FOUR

Annie's Plaid Shirt

Wendy Garay and Bethany Gonzales

Introduction

The book *Annie's Plaid Shirt* by Stacy B. Davids explores one of the complex issues parents and caregivers experience when navigating the tension between wanting children to be their authentic selves and having to deal with normative forms of gender expression.

In this lesson, students use the book to explore two key ideas: (1) allyship and (2) being able to feel like their authentic selves.

> "I'll definitely say the thing that impacted me the most at CSUB was running for homecoming king, and how they changed the labels with titles the following year. So as always, homecoming king and queen, when someone hears king, they automatically think of male and queen as a female, because in the following year, they did homecoming royalty. It was more inclusive. It was acknowledging transgender, nonbinary people who want to run. It showed that they want to be there for all identities, doesn't matter what. Just that big moment—to see that really boosted my self-esteem. Really made me feel like I can make a difference in the LGBTQ community. And I can make a difference, especially in Bakersfield, which still has a little bit of a rough time with LGBTQ. But just to see that change at a California State University, that quickly and in a year, I feel all universities, UCs, community colleges, they can all make that same difference."– V. Zepeda

Details

Topics/Curricular Connections
- Language Arts/Reading

Grade Level/Audience

- Grades 6 through 8

Learning Objectives

- Students will use details from the text to make connections and answer questions.
- Students are successful when they can answer questions in connection with the text.
- Students will use art and writing to respond to the question, "What outfit makes you feel like your most authentic self?"
- Students are successful when they can use writing to explain their choices.

Common Core Standards

- RL.6.1: Cite textual evidence to support analysis of what the text says explicitly as well as inferences drawn from the text.
- RL.6.3: Describe how a particular story's or drama's plot unfolds in a series of episodes as well as how the characters respond or change as the plot moves toward a resolution.
- RL.7.1: Cite several pieces of textual evidence to support analysis of what the text says explicitly as well as inferences drawn from the text.
- RL.7.3: Analyze how particular elements of a story or drama interact (e.g., how setting shapes the characters or plot).
- RL.8.1: Cite the textual evidence that most strongly supports an analysis of what the text says explicitly as well as inferences drawn from the text.
- RL.8.2: Determine a theme or central idea of a text and analyze its development over the course of the text, including its relationship to the characters, setting, and plot; provide an objective summary of the text.

Materials

- The book *Annie's Plaid Shirt* by Stacy B. Davids
- My Perfect Outfit Handout

Compelling Questions

- What outfit makes you feel like your most authentic self?
- How can you be a supportive friend, family member, and ally?

Supporting Questions

- What is an ally?
- Why is it essential to be an ally?

- How do allies make us feel?
- What can allies do to help?
- What makes your outfit awesome?
- How do awesome outfits make us feel?

Lesson Steps

This activity is designed to guide learning and understanding through group discussion and making inferences. Students will develop predictions based on the book cover, engage in discussion of the text, and apply their learning by completing an art activity.

Previewing the Book

As you display the book's cover, invite students to respond to the following pre-reading questions:

- What do you see happening on the cover of this book?
- Based on the cover, what do you think this book will be about? Why?

As you prepare to read the book out loud, define the term "ally" and the different ways people can be allies for students. Display the definition and description prominently, so students can refer back to them as you move through the lesson.

Reading Together

As you read the book aloud, offer the following questions when you encounter each related portion of the text:

1. Why do you think Annie always wears her plaid shirt? (p. 6)
2. What is Annie's facial expression telling us about how she might feel? (p. 12)
3. Have you ever had to wear something you did not want to? How did you feel? (p. 16)
4. After shopping, Annie runs to her room and slams the door. Why do you think she does that? How do you think she might be feeling? (p. 18)
5. When Annie's mother and brother have their discussion, what is Annie's mother worried about? Why do you think she would have such a worry? How do you think Annie would feel knowing her brother is sticking up for her? (p. 22)
6. Annie has a creative solution for her wedding outfit. What made it a good solution for the problem she was dealing with? (p. 28)

Deepening Inquiry into the Concept of Allyship

Once you've completed the read-aloud, you can invite students to use a thinking map or other process for responding to questions like:

- We explored the idea of being an ally before we began reading together. In the story, who was an ally for Annie?
- Why do you think it is important to be an ally to other people?
- How do allies make us feel?
- What are some examples of things that allies can do to help people facing difficulty?

> *"One of the things is your name. You're gonna go through so many names. And the one thing is, when someone accepts you, it's, 'Now you have to call me by what I feel: he/him, she/her, they/them, any preference.' And that's going to be, of course, a struggle for them. And I'm not gonna say it's not gonna be hard—it will be because you knew this person as this one person—but they're not any different, and I think that's the one thing that's not talked about is we're still the same person. You think that your daughter or son has died when really, it's just who they are. They're still that same child you birthed or that same friend you made back then. It's just the outer parts of themselves that they're coming to terms with. So, I think when it comes to acceptance, can you work on calling me by the name I want? The pronouns I want? Can you defend me when someone's like, 'Well, no, that's a girl' and be like, 'No, that's my son.' 'That's my best friend.' 'That's my brother.' You're going to get picked on, bullied, name-called, all that, and sometimes it happens in front of those same people, and the question is, are those same people going to stick up for you? Because you might not be able to do it for yourself? Or if you have, you're gonna become anxious, you're going to become defensive and emotional, and you're going to be frustrated? Can they support you in that situation?"* – D. Hughes

Making Personal Connections

In this activity, students design and write about an outfit that makes them feel like their authentic self. This is an opportunity for them to share their unique style and to showcase the diversity of styles represented in the classroom. Students can use the handout provided and/or draw an outfit of their own design.

Prime students with a prompt like:

"In the book, Annie felt 'happiest' in her plaid shirt and felt 'weird' wearing dresses. Sometimes we feel most happy, most comfortable, or most like ourselves in certain clothes. For example, I feel most like myself when I'm in sweatpants and a t-shirt:

- Think about an outfit that makes you feel happiest or most like your true self.
- Describe the outfit from top to bottom. Are there specific shoes? No shoes? A specific kind of garment like a skirt or hoodie? Are there accessories involved like hats, scarves, or earrings?
- Now draw your outfit!"

Teachers, feel free to offer suggestions for specific occasions if students hit a roadblock. For example, you can suggest going to a wedding, to the mall, to a concert, being at home, etc.

> "I think a lot of [celebrating T*GC community] is about how the difference is important and beautiful in many different ways. It challenges people to think of the world in a different way. If you look, historically, there are so many examples of individuals like this occupying positions of importance in society. It's clear that society values the insights that someone that lives in this liminal space could bring. There's someone who is not bound by the conventional rules, I guess you could say, in the same way that artists are celebrated because they think about life in a different way, and they're able to express it, and they're able to share that information with others. I think, just the mindset that you have, because of being trans* and navigating society, gives you insight into many other things that exist within society that don't necessarily have to exist the way that they exist, or it helps you see it through a lens that other people may not, and people value that wisdom.
>
> Recognition, and amplification, I think are kind of the main ones. I'm not super familiar with the academic terms around, but everything that you think of when it comes to celebration, around identities is also relevant here. And not just identities. People often think of parties or something like that, when you talk about celebration, and I think that you should do that. In the same way that we do have parties where we recognize other kinds of identities, and other kinds of people. We throw parties because artists have made a bunch of work. It's like, 'Okay, let's go to a gallery opening.' We can have similar kinds of recognition for trans* people that are talking about or are centered on their contributions, their insights, and their wisdom." – S. Javitz

Optional Discussion and Community Building

After students design their authentic outfits, you can invite them into a discussion. It's important to keep this optional and not make it a requirement, as some outfits and their stories may be personal or private. You can ask questions like:

- Who is willing to describe their outfit to the class?
- What was your inspiration for drawing this outfit?
- How does your outfit make you feel?
- How is your outfit authentically you?
- What's one thing you love most about your outfit?
- Where would you like to wear this outfit?

Closing Activity

Invite students to write a response to the prompts:

1. Everyone has a unique style, which is great! What outfit makes you feel like your most authentic self? Use the book, your artwork, and our class discussion to help you describe your outfit and what it says about you.
2. Sometimes we experience difficulty and need a helping hand. Think about a time when you were struggling. What happened? How could others have shown up as allies for you? (Or, if they did, what did they do?)

Applying the Three Guiding Frameworks

The Gender Identity Complexities Framework

There is a tension around gender norms and clothing in this book. Annie's mother states that "little girls always wear dresses to weddings" and tries to enforce this social rule with Annie, causing significant distress. The author lets us know that Annie's mother is worried about what other people will think. The implication is that there could be a negative social consequence to not conforming (and, in real life, there really can be).

It's Annie's brother, embodying sj Miller's Gender Identity Complexities Framework, who enables a compromise: Annie gets to wear her plaid shirt as part of a formal outfit, in this case a suit, not a dress. Annie's brother advocates for Annie's complex gender identity (*complexity*), actively supports her particular gender expression (*authenticity*), fully accepts Annie's self-definition, and creates space for Annie to push back against gender and gender identity constructs, challenge norms and stereotypes, and refuse the historical embedding of strict gender expectations in a religious ritual (*critical consciousness*).

The Bridge to Thriving Framework

With its focus on affirming authentic *selfhood*, both through the book and the subsequent activities, this lesson supports true belonging for students in a way that pushes back on gender norms and stereotypes (*community*, critical consciousness, *selfhood*). There is a kind of *abundance* in choosing to highlight Annie's story and then using it to invite students to express who they truly are, which has the potential to build students' hope and imagination about possibilities for themselves and others.

There are several ways that this lesson seeks to create a *pleasurable* experience for students: Annie's story has a happy ending, students have several opportunities to connect with each other in affirming ways, and they get to use art as an avenue for authentic self-expression in a context where their truth is welcome. All of this can also be a source of *relief*, particularly for students who have felt the need to hide aspects of their identities, who have been hungry for affirming classroom experiences, or who needed to see T*GC representation.

Annie's story, particularly its ending, offers a possibility model for *simply being*, or being able to exist fully as one's self—whole in mind, body, and spirit.

The Historically Responsive Literacy Framework

This lesson is designed to affirm students' *identities* (feeling like their authentic selves) while also modeling what it can look like to affirm the identity of a gender-creative young person. Annie's story writes people like her into students' understanding of T*GC history and responds to the need for inclusion and representation.

Becoming *skillful* scholars is key to Muhammad's framework. In this case, students practice close reading, discussion, making predictions and inferences, and making connections between the text and their lived experiences.

Through this lesson, students "become smarter about" engaging in creative allyship, T*GC experiences, and some of the tensions that exist around gender norms, including the interpersonal conflict they can cause and the potential for social consequences when people don't conform (*intellect, critical consciousness*). Middle school students will likely also empathize with Annie's feelings of powerlessness as her mother tried to force her to be someone she wasn't and do things that were out of alignment with her authentic self.

Finally, readers get to witness Annie's *joy* at being able to wear her plaid shirt in a way that aligns to the formality of a wedding. Her mother's and brother's affirmation and the resolution of conflict are a relief. The lesson is also intended to help students locate their own joyful self-expression through clothing that feels authentic to them.

References

Davids, S. B. (2015). *Annie's Plaid Shirt*. Upswing Press.

Davids, S. B. (2015). *Annie's Plaid Shirt* [Digital version]. https://docs.google.com/presentation/d/1LvJSuDIX-JwNrPPfr3hN4mCdu28p1BJlXCpFd9wHo-0/edit?usp=sharing

Garay, W., & Gonzales, B. (2023). *My perfect outfit handout*. https://drive.google.com/file/d/1ONZ8qNVP-qULmPE5xZhmSbb-fPIrSxoc/view?usp=drive_link

INTERLUDE ONE

"Just prior to high school and waking up to my own sexual interest in other girls, I remember my excitement at having discovered the theater! I auditioned for the high school production of The Music Man as an 8th grader and was cast in the chorus of River City children who joined the band. I realize now, as a fully grown adult, that this was the first time in my life and school career that I was socially allowed, encouraged even, to play with the girls.

Many of the kids drawn to music and dancing also happened to be smart and nerdy. They 'got' me and my sense of humor. I also think I gravitated toward drama, in general, and acting, specifically, because I sensed that it could allow me to be someone other than myself for a time, stepping out of my own anxieties and traumas and the roles put upon me by the expectations of my boy-shaped body.

I could put on a costume and strut differently, speak differently, be free of all my self-imposed limitations . . . and honestly, theater meant close proximity to the dazzling and alluring women's dresses, shoes, hats, and gloves in the costume shop—the stuff I really wanted to play with, but there were no roles available to justify putting a boy in a ball gown. Makeup, however, was required for everyone on stage.

I was enthralled, hooked, and transformed once I experienced the close intimacy, the tender care each girl on the crew would give to my face, and the enjoyment they had putting makeup on a boy who (I think) they sensed enjoyed it too. We were united in a common goal—making me gorgeous for the stage! I had a 6-word solo to sing after all.

I experienced a safe, socially acceptable, however fleeting space to simply enjoy the fun of makeup, together, right there in the choir room after school. It was the first time I felt a sense of caring feminine sisterhood in my body. My new goal of joining the elite choir and starring in every play and musical I could once I got to high school suddenly became a biological imperative.

Of course, in reality, the theater department was (and likely still is) split along bi-gendered lines, with separate dressing rooms, women's roles for girls, and men's roles for boys. The 'variety of me' still had little sense of belonging, but I mostly behaved how boy-bodies were expected. At least theater held a sense of openness and play, of messing around with our appearances and identities, that allowed me some breathing room to express myself.

Theatre also gifted me with daily association with girls outside the classroom, enough to actually befriend them and begin, in their reflection, to build my own blossoming toward the feminine. Not much of the identity formation was conscious at the time, and definitely intertwined with blossoming sexual desires brought on by floods *of testosterone, not to mention being experienced completely without support, positive images, or role models, or even any vocabulary to describe my experience. Somehow, I made it through because of the 'good and crazy people,' my friends in the choir.*

Home wasn't safe to discuss my desires toward the feminine, but at least in the theater department, I felt like I had some kind of "home" in my wider, scarier high school existence, a place to go and a community where I could be more of myself—whatever I felt that day—and it was cool." – K. James

CHAPTER FIVE

Be You!

Ana Cornejo

Introduction

THIS LESSON IS A precursor activity to reading the book *Melissa* by Alex Gino. Some educators call this process "interviewing the book." The lesson invites students to reflect on the experiences of a marginalized character while also reflecting on their own experiences through a variety of discussion questions. The goal is to create a path to community, communication, and action in the classroom and beyond.

Details

Topics/Curricular Connections
- Social Emotional Learning
- Reading/Language Arts

Grade Level/Audience
- Grade 4 and up

Learning Objectives
- Participants are provided with opportunities to drive their learning experiences through empathy and compassion by connecting to a marginalized character, reflecting on their own experiences, and calling to action by suggesting solutions.
- Through leveled questions, discussion questions, and the Think Pair Share strategy, participants have opportunities to get to know and value each other's experiences, contributions, and opinions.

Common Core Standards

- CCSS.ELA-Literacy.SL.4.1, 5.1: Engage effectively in a range of collaborative discussions (one-on-one, in groups, and teacher led) with diverse partners on grade 4 (5) topics and texts, building on others' ideas and expressing their own clearly.
- CCSS.ELA-Literacy.RL.4.1, 5.1: Refer to details and examples (quote accurately) in a text when explaining what the text says explicitly and when drawing inferences from the text.
- CCSS.ELA-Literacy.L.4.1, 5.1: Demonstrate command of the conventions of standard English grammar and usage when writing or speaking

Materials

- Book: *Melissa* by Alex Gino
- Supplies: poster-size construction paper, colored pencils, pencils, markers, crayons
- Journals

Compelling Questions

- What do you think it means to be who you are?
- What actions can we take in our classroom to ensure that we all feel like we belong?

Lesson Duration

- Discussion 10–15 min
- Art project 2–4 days

Pedagogical Notes

It is recommended that teachers be prepared to discuss trans* and gender-creative identities, as well as challenges that T*GC community members face, like being excluded and misunderstood. Here are some resources to support having such conversations:

- Toilets, bowties, gender and me | Audrey Mason-Hyde | TEDx Adelaide (video)
- How to Support Transgender Students | GLSEN (video)
- How to Build Safe & Inclusive Schools for Trans*+ & Gender-Creative Youth (video)
- GLSEN Ready Set Respect - A critical thinking toolkit with lessons.
- Talking to Young Children About Gender | Gender Spectrum – A flier with key concepts and tips, as well as questions to help adults understand what children already think and know about gender.

- Gender & Sexual Identity | Learning for Justice – A collection of resources about sex assigned at birth, sexual orientation, gender identity and gender expression, and learning how to advocate for LGBTQ youth.
- Expressing Myself. My Way. – An animated video offering definitions of key terms and examples of gender identity and expression across different scenarios.
  - *Note:* At 1:37 min, the term "sex" is defined as "what you are labeled when you are born, usually boy or girl." Students might need a reminder that the term can have multiple meanings.

Lesson Steps

Activating Prior Knowledge

Ask students what they know about *sympathy, empathy, compassion*, and *belonging*.

- Collect student ideas about what they think each term means and how it might look, what it might feel like, and how it could be expressed. Teachers can invite students to co-construct definitions, draw representative images, put ideas on big paper on the wall, or whatever feels vibrant.
- Next, help students refine their understanding of these terms, perhaps using the resources provided below:
  - Brené Brown on "Fitting in" vs. "Belonging" (brief video)
  - Brené Brown on Empathy vs. Sympathy (brief video)
  - Empathy vs. Compassion (brief video)

Introducing the Book

- Introduce the book *Melissa* by showing its cover image and pose the following question:
  - Based on the cover, what do you think this book will be about?
  - Why? What clues and prior knowledge are you using to make this prediction?
  - [*Sentence Frame: Based on the cover, I think the book is about _____ because _____.*]
  - Provide thinking time and then ask students to share their predictions with their shoulder partners or peers near them.
- Once students have had time for discussion, ask for volunteers to share with the group.
  - Possible sentence frames for students that learn best with visual cues:
    - Based on the cover, my partner and I think the book is about _____ because _____.
    - Based on the cover, my partner thinks the book is about _____, and I agree because _____.

- ▪ Based on the cover, my partner thinks the book is about _____, and I respectfully disagree because _____.
- Provide students with a written copy or the book itself and read the blurb on the back cover of the book out loud:
  - "When people look at Melissa, they think they see a boy. But she knows she's not a boy. She knows she's a girl. Melissa thinks she'll have to keep this a secret forever. Then her teacher announces that their class play is going to be *Charlotte's Web*. Melissa really, really, REALLY wants to play Charlotte. But the teacher says she can't even try out for the part . . . because she's a boy. With the help of her best friend, Kelly, Melissa comes up with a plan. Not just so she can be Charlotte—but so everyone can know who she is, once and for all."
- Invite students to offer a new prediction:
  - Now that we have read the blurb, how would you update your prediction of what this book is about?
  - What do you think Melissa's plan might be?
  - What could someone in Melissa's position do?

> *"It is the exposure to the different narratives that are out there. The real exposure is not just a job for the schools, this is a job for society, in general. But schools can put an interesting spin on it and can kind of present media that is created by trans* people, etc., to give people this idea, somewhere to head off, in terms of what they want to do in their free time, research, whatever you want to call it but to explicitly create that space to talk about these identities and how they differ and what's there. I think, in general, we don't do this super well. We're doing a better job on this, by creating spaces for people to explore these identities. But I'm just thinking back on my own education, and how many Black people did I learn about in school? And what was the framework through which it was presented? Because it's not flattering. We need to do a better job at presenting this diversity of narrative experience."* – S. Javitz

Deepening Student Inquiry

- Introduce some context and history about being a trans* or gender-creative student. (Several resources are provided above.)
- You can use the Think Pair Share strategy to pose the following discussion questions as you deepen students' inquiry:
  - Why do you think Melissa thinks she'll have to keep who she really is a secret?
    - ▪ *Possible sentence frame*: I think Melissa thinks she'll have to keep who she really is a secret because _____.
  - How do you think Melissa feels about her teacher not allowing her to try out for the part of Charlotte?

BE YOU!

- ■ *Possible sentence frame*: I think Melissa feels _____ about her teacher not allowing her to try out for the part of Charlotte because _____.
- – Can you think of a time when you could not participate in an activity because of who you are? How did that make you feel?
  - ■ *Possible sentence frame*: A time I could not participate in activity was when _____. I felt_____.
- – (Empathy and compassion) What do you think it means to be who you are? (It's okay if you don't have an answer or don't know yet.)
  - ■ *Possible sentence frame*: I think to be who you are means _____.

> "From the top down, [theatre] gave that feel. It definitely gave that flair. With the students, it was very representative of our world. Queer people usually find our way to the theater. I would say it was very far and few between, but for the most part, it was. Now it wasn't a talked about thing, but it was 'I'm in class and I'm with my boy friends.' It's very normal. In high school hallways, students make out and do other crazy things. If it's a girl and a boy, 'Girl get to class, boy go to class.' Boy and a boy?: 'Boy go to class.' It was across the board. I was definitely cocooned. And I'm realizing more and more today that, yes, it was a very accepting environment. Now, if we looked at it in today's time, it probably would not be. I would say for the time that we were in, it was as accepting as it could be." – Benjamin

Application of Learning

Invite students to complete an art project that will help others develop sympathy, empathy, or compassion.

- Option 1: Create a poster that could be used to showcase and promote Melissa in the role of Charlotte for the play.
- Option 2: During the discussion, it was asked if you could think of a time when you could not participate in an activity because of who you are. Create a poster illustrating your participation in the previously denied activity.

At the conclusion of the lesson, organize a gallery walk so that students can experience one another's work.

- Teachers can provide sticky notes and encourage students to record Wows (what you noticed or stood out to you) and Wonders (what you're curious about related to the artwork).
- Students can leave the sticky notes near the artwork or keep them.
- As students conclude the gallery walk, post the following journal prompts:
  - What do you think it means to be who you are?
  - Why are sympathy, empathy, and compassion important in relationships?

- What actions can we take in our classroom to ensure that we all feel like we belong?

Possible sentence frames:

- I think to be who you are means _____.
- Empathy and compassion are important in relationships because_____.
- Actions I can take in our classroom to ensure that we all feel like we belong are _____. Strategies to ensure we all feel like we belong are _____.

Applying the Three Guiding Frameworks

The Gender Identity Complexities Framework

The act of sharing Melissa's story with students in a heteronormative setting is an act of advocacy. In addition, students are being exposed to the *complexity* of gender identities by reflecting on their own experiences and the experiences of others. Furthermore, *authenticity* and various and multiple means of gender and expressing of gender identity are supported through facilitated discussions. *Self-definition* is practiced by students as they are invited to reflect on their experiences, as well as Melissa's. The lesson encourages *critical consciousness* as students explore, engage, and push back against gender identity constructs by advocating for themselves and others through discussion, artistic expression, and imagining greater belonging for all.

The Bridge to Thriving Framework

This lesson calls for exploration of students' personal stories, providing opportunities for students to get to know and value each other's contributions and opinions, which develops a sense of *community*. Students' reflections on their own journeys can allow them to affirm their *authentic selves*. Participants can also experience *abundance* through opportunities to drive their learning experiences by connecting to a marginalized character, reflecting on their own experiences, and calling for action by suggesting solutions. Discussion questions are written in a way so that there are no right or wrong answers. Social-Emotional Learning can help reduce stress among students by developing self-awareness, self-management, social awareness, relationship skills, and responsible decision-making and thus provide a sense of *relief*. Lastly, the lesson can provide students with a sense that people can exist fully or *simply be*, which is present through Melissa's story. In addition, participants can share their experiences with a similar situation, thus honoring participants holistically.

The Historically Responsive Literacy Framework

Participants learn about anti-oppression through Melissa's story and are encouraged to learn about *identity* through reflection questions. In addition, participants build their literacy and language *skills* through engaging in meaningful conversations with their peers. The lesson also builds upon participants' *intellect*, knowledge, and mental powers through their reflections, discussions, and sharing of experiences. Participants also engage *critically* in the disruption of oppression by both recognizing it and imagining belonging. Lastly, the instruction elevates *joy* in humanity by encouraging participants to share their truth and be who they are while empowering others to do the same.

References

Amaze.org. (2016, October 5). *Expressing myself. My way* [Video]. YouTube. https://www.youtube.com/watch?v=ITRdvGnplLU

Barajas, V. (2020, September 18). *Empathy v. compassion* [Video]. YouTube. https://www.youtube.com/watch?v=pjDu_7xGy6w

Brown, B. (2021, July 26). *This is what true belonging means* [Video]. Wealth4Well. https://www.youtube.com/watch?v=HoJYe8wbi24

eMINTS Professional Learning. (2021). *Shoulder partner discussion.* University of Missouri College of Education and Human Development. https://sites.google.com/a/emints.org/cooperative-learning-strategies/shoulder-partner-discussion

Francis-Sears, A., & Stephenson, A. (2016, April 1). *Brené Brown on empathy v. sympathy* [Video]. Royal Society of Arts. https://www.youtube.com/watch?v=KZBTYViDPlQ

Gender Spectrum. (2017). *Talking to young children about gender.* https://gender-spectrum.cdn.prismic.io/gender-spectrum/632688b7-b250-4bea-8f41-ffffddc2834f_Talking+to+Young+Kids+flyer+8.25.17+final.pdf

Gino, A. (2022). *Melissa.* Scholastic Press.

GLSEN. (2017, November 13). *How to support transgender students* [Video]. YouTube. https://www.youtube.com/watch?v=kq19QdOfH1Y

Learning for Justice. (n.d.). *Gender & sexual identity.* Southern Poverty Law Center. https://www.learningforjustice.org/topics/gender-sexual-identity?gclid=Cj0KCQjwla-hBhD7ARIsAM9tQKtW9M0auZYKrW1UgJqfD_8dH4I6cNv0evCM3fbRvuTT1zShYrf_4GsaAvanEALw_wcB

Mason-Hyde, A. (2018, January 19). *Toilets, bowties, gender and me* [Video]. TEDx Adelaide. https://www.youtube.com/watch?v=NCLoNwVJA-0

McGarry, R.A., Friedman, L., Bouley, T., & Griffin, P. (2016). *Ready, set, respect: GLSEN's elementary school toolkit.* GLSEN. https://www.glsen.org/sites/default/files/GLSEN%20Ready%20Set%20Respect.pdf

PCG. (2017, October 25). *How to build safe and inclusive schools for trans*+ & gender-creative youth* [Video]. YouTube. https://www.youtube.com/watch?v=ryV6lI1pawI

Teach For Life. (2018, September 20). *Think pair share.* https://www.youtube.com/watch?v=Mig4olzUy4M

CHAPTER SIX

Exploring Identity and Selfhood

Shaylyn Marks

Introduction

In this unit, students use pre-reading activities, reflective journaling, discussion, and their own memoir writing to engage with the memoir *All Boys Aren't Blue* by George M. Johnson (they/them), exploring how personal and social identities are shaped and, in turn, shape who we are. This lesson encourages students to use writing as a tool for reflecting about identity, intersectionality, and the art of writing itself.

I hope that by the end of the unit, students will have a greater understanding of their own identities, others' identities, and how identities interact with the larger society. This is designed to be a pathway for students to cultivate deeper compassion, empathy, community, and abundance—both for themselves and for others.

> "First of all, I think about representation. That's kind of the bare minimum of celebration. To be able to see it at all. Not something that I have been accustomed to, or that I think a lot of previous generations have had access to. But when I think about celebrating beyond the bare minimum, I think about the opportunity for trans* and gender non-conforming people to be able to share their stories, and for those stories to be heard by other people from their perspectives, rather than always having stories told about us. To have us being able to tell our own stories, and then have people actually connect to those because they can see that we're real people. I think that ownership of our own stories, and being able to connect to people, as other people, would probably be the kind of first thought for celebration." – B. Matthews

Details

Topics/Curricular Connections

- Reading

- Language Arts
- Social Emotional Learning

Grade Level/Audience

- Grade 9 and up

Social Emotional Learning Objectives

- Students will be able to reflect on the various facets of their identity and develop an understanding of how their multiple identities shape who they are.
- Students will be able to reflect on how society shapes our identities.
- Students will begin to cultivate an understanding of intersectionality.
- Students will develop compassion and empathy for themselves and others.

Common Core Standards

- CCR.1 - Read closely to determine what the text says explicitly and to make logical inferences from it; cite specific textual evidence when writing or speaking to support conclusions drawn from the text.
- CCR.2 - Determine central ideas or themes of a text and analyze their development; summarize the key supporting details and ideas.
- CCR.10 - Read and comprehend complex literary and informational texts independently and proficiently.
- CCW.3 - Write narratives to develop real or imagined experiences or events using effective technique, well-chosen details, and well-structured event sequences.
- CCW.4 - Produce clear and coherent writing in which the development, organization, and style are appropriate to task, purpose, and audience.
- CCW.5 - Develop and strengthen writing as needed by planning, revising, editing, rewriting, or trying a new approach.

Materials

- *All Boys Aren't Blue* by George M. Johnson
- Journal/notebook
- Computer access (typing memoirs)
- Art materials (for gallery walk presentations)

Compelling Questions

- How do various facets of our identity shape us as individuals?
- How does society influence and/or shape our identities?
- How can writing be used as a tool for reflection, self-exploration, and social emotional development?

EXPLORING IDENTITY AND SELFHOOD

Lesson Duration

This unit was written with 50-min class periods in mind and could span 4 weeks. This assumes students will do some reading and writing for homework.

Pedagogical Notes

Creating a Learning Container

I strongly encourage teachers to co-construct norms with students that create a safe environment for reflection, sharing, and growth, before engaging in discussion. Relatedly, some of the discussion topics could be considered sensitive and students may at times feel uncomfortable sharing all of their thoughts. Teachers are encouraged to let students know that they are in control of what they decide to say and can keep things private at their discretion. Journals may be a great place for students to express thoughts and feelings that they don't want to share aloud. It is important to respect students' personal boundaries and allow them time and space to unpack their ideas and identities in a safe, nurturing environment.

Please note that this memoir contains sexual content. Teachers are urged to review the text with an eye to their students' readiness to engage with it.

> *"In schools in general, in life, in the world. In schools, the goal is to make certain that kids feel seen, safe, and loved. I think I would start within our current world, just existing is, in some ways, its own celebration. Just existing as resistance. I think there's something about community for celebrating—ways of connecting, and being, and existing. I think there's something about knowing our history. Knowing our non-biological, trans* ancestors, families, connections. If we're talking schools, I think celebrating would include making certain that trans* people are seen in all of our multitudes and all of our joyful, messy mix. Stuff not mixed in a bad way, but the diversity way, selves and curriculum, in school, in leadership, in positions, in parents, and all the above. I think there's something about making time to exist and be in space and in our bodies. And picking places where I find the most trans* joy. My personal favorite is the queer, trans*, historically Black/Brown/QTPOC . . . choose your term . . . beach in Queens. It's the furthest end of the furthest New York City public beach. As far as you can get away as possible. And it's a lovely, joyful party."* – A. Daniels

Instruction & Assessment

This is a literary analysis unit and, while I have included some scaffolding, I haven't explored every concept deeply. I invite teachers to make use of additional tools that support literary inquiry.

I encourage teachers to rotate and join different literature and writing circle groups each day as a powerful way to understand students' developing learning. For this unit, the focus is on students' ability to use and build on concepts like identity, intersectionality, and story-writing.

Lesson Steps

As students engage with this unit about *All Boys Aren't Blue*, they will explore the concept of intersectionality[1] through the lens of Johnson's experiences, while critically examining their own identities, how their multifaceted identities make them who they are, and how society perceives them and others. Students will make use of literature circle groups[2] and whole class discussion, as well as reflective journaling[3] throughout the unit.

Activating Prior Knowledge

Activating prior knowledge before entering a story world is critical to helping students make connections between what they have already experienced and what they will encounter in the text and the larger unit. This opens up pathways for deeper learning.

- To activate prior knowledge and engage students before reading, students will participate in a five-minute quick write in their reflective journals with the following prompt: "List words to describe your identities."
  - The teacher can scaffold thinking about identity by first defining what "identity" means and the differences between a social vs. a personal identity.[4]
  - The teacher might consider using a Social Identity Wheel[5] activity to ground students' thinking.
  - The teacher can also pose reflection questions like: "Who are you?" "What makes you unique?" "How would you describe yourself?" and/or "Who are you in different contexts, like with your friends vs. at home vs. out in the community vs. when you're by yourself?"
- Then, students will share what they have written, which can both foster a welcoming environment and help peers generate additional ideas.
- The teacher will then ask students to reflect on their self-descriptions:
  - Are there similarities/differences in the words you chose to describe yourself?
  - Could you categorize the words you used into larger groups of related words?
  - Is anything missing?
  - How do these words work together to begin describing your identity(ies)?
  - Are there words on your list that you feel more comfortable sharing than others?
  - Which parts of your identity were chosen by other people or by society for you?
  - Which parts of your identity did you choose for yourself?

Exploring Identity Complexity

- Students will participate in an "I Am"[6] poem writing exercise, where they create a poem using the identity descriptors above, their personal histories, and "I am" sentence frames.
  - A powerful practice is to invite students to share their poems, then collect and hang them around the classroom to validate each student's identity and serve as inspiration as they read, then write their memoirs.
- The teacher will guide students toward understanding that identity is multifaceted using a Personal Identity Wheel activity.[7]
  - First, students will take 5–7 min to think about their *personal* identities, completing the Identity Wheel as a guide.
  - Then, students can share their observations (small or whole groups).
  - The teacher can scaffold their thinking with questions like:
    - How did your sense of who you are or what identities you hold change as you used the Identity Wheel?
    - Were there components of your identity that were harder to share? [Please see Pedagogical Notes above]
    - Can anyone share the skill they are proud of?
    - Who would like to share the three adjectives they used to describe themselves?
    - Can anyone share their motto?
    - What are some of the things you have in common with each other?
- The teacher will introduce the concept of "intersectionality," which "refers to the social, economic, and political ways in which identity-based systems of oppression and privilege connect, overlap and influence one another."[8] In other words, intersectionality describes the unique burdens that are created when multiple oppressions—like being *both* Black *and* a woman in a racist and misogynistic society, or being disabled *and* transgender *and* an immigrant—compound one another to create a new and particular kind of oppression. Inviting reflection on the many ways identity can manifest and/or intersect, the teacher can ask:
  - Which, if any, of your *personal* identities are informed by your *social* identities (age, race, gender, sex, etc.)?
  - Are there certain places/spaces where one part of your identity is more or less prominent? If so, why do you think that is?
  - Consider the various identifiers you have described in your journals; how do these potentially intersect or build upon one another? For example, being both Asian and a girl is a different experience from being both Asian and gender nonbinary—talk about how your identities interact.
  - Think about how a combination of two oppressed identities might create burdens that are specific to being a person with *both* of those identities. What examples come to mind? What are their unique challenges?

Introducing the Text

- The teacher will introduce *All Boys Aren't Blue* to students by connecting it to the pre-reading activities and inviting students to predict what the book will be about.
- The teacher will then read the first section of Act I, Chapter 1 to students and set a purpose for reading before allowing students to read independently for the remainder of the class period.
  - *The Purpose for Reading* – As students read the first act, invite them to consider: (i) the various facets of George's identity; (ii) how these facets build upon one another, intersect, or conflict; and (iii) how society potentially shapes George's identity (or elements of their identity).

Working Through the Text

Students will read each Act, one at a time, use their reflective journals, and have discussions in their literature circle groups. As groups complete each Act, the teacher can pull them back together as a whole class to share their reflections, observations, and questions. The teacher can be attuned to understanding of the text and growing awareness around students' identities, others' identities, and questions of power and intersectionality.

Guiding Questions and Journal Prompts for Act 1

- Identify characteristics or facets of George's identity using evidence from the text to support your claims. What are some of George's *social* identities? What are some of George's *personal* identities?
- Find an example of where multiple facets of George's identity intersect or interact. Cite textual evidence to support your claim.
- In Chapter 1, the author states, "The trauma is shared by the community, too" (p. 32). Can you think of an example where a community of people share trauma? Explain.
- Chapter 2 introduces readers to the idea of "agency." How do you define agency? Based on George's and/or your definition of agency, how do you see agency used in a real-world setting (this could be a personal experience, something you've witnessed in others, or something that you have seen depicted in a fictional world such as a book or movie).
- Based on your definition of agency (and perhaps George's definition), how might agency relate to personal and social identity?
- The author states, "Your name is one of the most important pieces of your identity ... Your name holds power when you walk into a room" (p. 49). How does the story of George's name relate to their identity? Think about someone who has a name with a story attached to it (this person could be you, and the name

EXPLORING IDENTITY AND SELFHOOD

could be a nickname, a last name, a first name, etc.). What is the story of that name? How does the name reflect, empower, or support that person's identity?
- How does society support or reject George's identity? Cite textual evidence to explain your claims.

Guiding Questions and Journal Prompts for Act 2

- George seems to have an exterior and an interior identity. How do these identities differ? Why do they only share parts of their identity with their family and friends? How does the author help readers understand George's values and goals around what they share, when, and with whom?
- The author states, "Your name is one of the most important pieces of your identity . . . Your name holds power when you walk into a room" (p. 49). How does the story of George's name relate to their identity? Think about someone who has a name with a story attached to it (this person could be you, and the name could be a nickname, a last name, a first name, etc.). What is the story of that name? How does the name reflect, empower, or support that person's identity?
- How does society support or reject George's identity? Cite textual evidence to explain your claims.

Guiding Questions and Journal Prompts for Act 3

- Multiple times throughout the text, George reflects on people who have served as role models for them. Who is a role model for you? How has this person influenced your life? Explain.
- Throughout the text thus far, there are multiple instances where George describes how people, media, and society at large work to accept and/or reject facets of their identity. Look back at your preliminary journaling regarding your identity. How have people, media, society, etc., worked to: (a) accept, (b) reject, and (c) shape your identity?

Guiding Questions and Journal Prompts for Act 4

- How does George work to disrupt and/or reject societal norms and influences on identity? How do George's attempts to disrupt and/or reject societal norms reflect their acceptance and affirmation of their personal identity?
- How can you disrupt societal norms and influences on identity to provide relief and selfhood (including identity affirmation) for yourself and/or others?
- What is the overarching theme of the memoir? Support your claim with evidence and elaborate.
- Now that you have completed the book, describe George's personal journey with regard to their identities. What changed or evolved? What stayed the same? What did they learn?

- How does the author's choice to use memoir style writing impact the development of plot and theme?

Writing Personal Memoirs

This stage of the unit is a short memoir assignment in which students pick one pivotal event from their lives to write about. Students can use their notes and journaling to support memoir brainstorming and writing. Thus, they demonstrate the transfer of their reading comprehension skills into writing (identifying the main idea → developing the main idea, etc.). As inspiration, refer back to the book's introduction where the author quotes Toni Morrison saying, "If there's a book that you want to read, but it hasn't been written yet, then you must write it" (p. 14).[9]

- Prompt students to review their notes and journals with an eye to identifying a significant moment or memory in their own lives to write about.
- Scaffolding writing:
  - Engage students in a Five Senses Brainstorm as they revisit that moment/memory to recall what they saw, heard, smelled, tasted, and felt at the time.
  - Invite them to think about which of their identities—personal and social—were activated during the event.
  - Invite them to think about power dynamics that might have been playing out during the event and intersectionality.
  - Invite them to think about who else might have been present during the event and how they might have perceived it.
- Turn the student literature circle groups into writing groups so that students can continue conversing and sharing with peers familiar with their reflective journey. Give students time to collaborate and brainstorm to begin the writing process, as well as drafting time and small group time to discuss and revise as much as needed.

> *"I would think about in these like, big, vibrant, thriving moments, just the absolute power of community, how lonely and exhausting it is to be the one. And there are so many places in the world and in our country and in our communities, where people are just the one or the few. And how much power there is, and how much love and actualization and agency comes from community. Even if it's a small but mighty community, I would not be here without my community and I don't know many queer people who can say that they would be without that chosen family, like your ride or die folks, that are by your side. No matter what, I think a really important piece—like the foundation—is that vibrant, thriving community. None of us would be the person you see at Pride who everybody wants to be . . . that person didn't get there alone. The most flamboyant, amazing, entertaining, loving community member that you know, didn't become that person alone. We could all be that person, if only we could harness the power of our community and didn't have to focus so much on just surviving."* – B. Kennedy

Memoir Art

Upon completing their memoir writing, give students a few days to create an artistic representation of their work (sketches, drawings, collage, or other media), then exhibit their memoirs and art in a gallery walk.

Applying the Three Guiding Frameworks

The Gender Identity Complexities Framework

A central theme of *All Boys Aren't Blue* is the author's evolving gender identity and expression, including having an alter ego modeled after Olympic gymnast Dominique Dawes and "gravitat[ing] toward [girls] because they were a reflection of what [George] was feeling inside" (p. 55). Exploring the author's struggles and journey encourages fruitful conversation with students about how social factors influence gender identity as well as the hardships people can face when their identity does not match societal norms.

The selection of this text by this author opens an invitation for students to grapple with the *complexity* of gender identities and performances beyond binary norms, as well as the power of *self-definition*. Throughout the book, readers bear witness to Johnson's multiple performances of gender across various contexts, noting those that are *authentic* and those that are a matter of survival. Students engage with intersectionality and oppression around gender norms throughout this unit, building *critical consciousness* and imagining ways to push back against limiting constructs, stereotypes, and abuse.

The Bridge to Thriving Framework

By co-creating discussion norms, using sustained, collaborative reading and writing circles, and engaging in meaningful reflection, this unit is designed to build students' sense of *community*, as well as their compassion and empathy for others, even beyond the classroom. Focusing on both reading and writing memoirs, along with explicit exploration of identity lends itself to developing a sense of *selfhood* and anchoring student's work in George M. Johnson's memoir, specifically, will help them identify tools for disrupting societal norms that cause harm and reimagine the world (*abundance*). All of this together can help students feel a sense of *abundance* and *relief*, as they become more connected, more critically conscious, more grounded, and better equipped to disrupt societal pressures when needed. The hope is that students move towards a state of *simply being* where they feel safe, loved, and appreciated for being who they are.

> **Content Warning:** The vignette below contains mention of suicide.

> "I think, if anything, if someone were to take away from this and anything that I said, mental health is going to be your number one priority . . . I wish I had my mental health intact before I had figured out who I was. I still struggle to this day. You know acceptance and support is the most important thing because I went through life alone on everything. Didn't meet my girlfriend until high school and didn't have that support till late high school. So, imagine just a child. I entered this all very depressed and alone. And I wasn't loved, I didn't know what that was, I was just doing my thing, and . . . very, very difficult. It's hard. Was very suicidal for a very long time.
>
> Some people aren't gonna understand what you're going through. I still feel very alone a lot of the time, so I'd say support is the biggest thing that you can get, and kind of just reminding that person that you're there and that you love them. Because if you could read their mind, sometimes you'd shed tears because a person could really think that way of themselves that there's so little, that their breath isn't worth it. Because it's so difficult. I'm trying to understand life and things. And be okay. And sometimes all you need is that reassurance and that reminder that they're there. Because it's so hard to tell someone: 'I'm struggling,' because you don't want to make that person feel bad. And I think being trans* adds to that because in society we are deemed as a phase or bad things and then we get killed for it. My mom used to tell me all the time when I first came out. Look, this person died. But I really just started living as myself." – D. Hughes

The Historically Responsive Literacy Framework

A key focus of this unit is *identity* exploration. In traditional classrooms, students rarely have opportunities to read beyond the literary canon and may not get to explore texts at the intersection of gender, sexuality, and self-exploration. This is particularly important now, as states ban books. The unit also encourages identity affirmation through the centering of students' personal histories and inherent genius.

Throughout this unit, students are encouraged to think critically about who they are, what makes them who they are, what makes the author who they are, how society influences people's identities and lives, and power and intersectionality (*criticality*).

Students build *skills* and *intellectualism* using reflective writing, formal composition (memoir), discussion, and literary analysis tied to the Common Core Standards. Finally, *joy* can be found in the empathetic and understanding community being built, in the honest conversations that center humanity and hone empowering skills, in the opportunity to tell powerful stories and create powerful art, and in the presence of a visionary text.

Notes

1. Crenshaw, 2017
2. For guides and resources on literature circles, please see Laura Candler's *How to Lead a Literature Circle*.

3. This allows students to not only reflect on what they have read but also to re-engage with the text before any class discussions/activities.
4. See Pabdoo, n.d.a and Pabdoo, n.d.b
5. See Pabdoo, n.d.b
6. A template and completed examples can be found at ReadWriteThink.
7. See Pabdoo, n.d.a
8. Gaffney et al., 2016
9. Additional sample memoirs that can be used with students include *Fish Cheeks* by Amy Tan, and those found in *Brevity* Magazine and *Hippocampus* Magazine.

References

Alber, R. (2016, December 06). *Enliven class discussions with gallery walks*. Edutopia. https://www.edutopia.org/blog/enliven-class-discussion-with-gallery-walks-rebecca-alber

Barbour, B. (2019, August 29). *The power of short writing assignments*. Edutopia. https://www.edutopia.org/article/power-short-writing-assignments

Brevity Magazine. (n.d.). *Home*. https://brevitymag.com/

Candler, L. (n.d.) *How to lead a literature circle*. https://www.lauracandler.com/wp-content/uploads/2018/06/circle.pdf

CommonLit. (n.d.) *Fish cheeks*. https://www.commonlit.org/en/texts/fish-cheeks

Crenshaw, K. (2017). *On intersectionality: Essential writings*. The New Press.

Gaffney, C., Mattingly, E., & Pettway, A. (2016). Teaching at the intersections. *Learning for Justice* (Summer). https://www.learningforjustice.org/magazine/summer-2016/teaching-at-the-intersections

Hippocampus Magazine. (n.d.). *Home*. https://hippocampusmagazine.com/

Johnson, G. M. (2020). *All boys aren't blue*. Penguin Books.

Journey Cloud. (n.d.). *Reflective journal*. https://journey.cloud/reflective-journal

Pabdoo. (n.d.a). *Personal identity wheel*. Inclusive Teaching. https://sites.lsa.umich.edu/inclusive-teaching/personal-identity-wheel/

Pabdoo. (n.d.b). *Social identity wheel*. Inclusive Teaching. https://sites.lsa.umich.edu/inclusive-teaching/social-identity-wheel/

ReadWriteThink.org (n.d.). *Writing an "I am" poem*. https://www.readwritethink.org/sites/default/files/resources/lesson_images/lesson391/I-am-poem.pdf

Ready, Set... Brainstorm! (n.d.). *Brainstorming method #3: The five senses*. http://readysetbrainstorm.weebly.com/the-five-senses.html

INTERLUDE TWO

What Are You Waiting For?: A Short Story

EL CHEN

The Stranger

Sprawling out on my pink sheets, I stare at them in disgust and frustration. *I despise this color. Why does Mom always buy everything in pink?* Out of the corner of my eye, I notice a pink ribbon lying on the floor, peeking out from my closet. *What is this doing here?* My chest heaves with quickening breaths. I clench my fists. Stomping to the closet, I pick up the bow and chuck it across my room. "Why does Mom keep all of my old stuff," I yell.

"Janus, I'm trying to study. Can you please tone it down a little?" my sister hollers. I walk across the hall, into her room, and chuck the pink bow at her.

"SHUT UP," I yell. My voice strains and tears form in my eyes. I run back to my room in a fury, my steps thudding with each heavy step. I collapse onto my ugly, pink bed. "I'm sorry," I whisper my apologies to her. I want to be louder, but I don't want to talk to her. "Why am I like this? Why am I so angry? I want to stop but I can't—" my voice cracks as I continue to whisper through tears to myself.

BAM! The closet door opens abruptly. A man, tall and lanky, topples into my room. His hair, dark brown with a blond streak, is in a messy bun. Dirt covers his face.

"Ouch, that hurt," he says as he sits up. He looks up and greets me, "Hi."

I'm speechless; a random, filthy man (who for some reason has hair just like mine) just fell out of my closet. *Where in the world did he come from?*

"Sorry for the unannounced visit, but you need to come with me," he announces, grabbing my arm. I feel frozen. I think of running but my feet refuse to move. He pulls me to the closet.

"For your safety, please keep your hands, arms, and legs within the vehicle," he announces in a monotonous voice, chuckling before chucking me. I soar through the closet wall, and everything goes black.

The Stranger Is Not a Stranger

I awake in a house built into nature. Sequoia trees melt into the house; the walls and ceiling are made out of wood, the grass beneath me lush, succulent, and sweet. Elevated above the ground, the view consists of miles of other trees in its surroundings. The startling rustling woke me, came from beyond the trees. In fear, I jump up to my feet and raise my arms and hands in a fist. The man that abducted me emerges through the forest wall. Vibrant green leaves and sticks in his hair. He holds a bottle with a crimson liquid.

"Well good morning, sleepyhead," the man says with a smile as he moved toward me. I flinch away. He chuckles before saying, "You're skittish. Guess you haven't come out yet. Well, don't worry. You'll come out to be a fine man." He points to himself. A large grin stretches across his face, revealing his pearly white teeth.

My hands shake as sweat beads from my forehead. *How did I not notice this stranger is me?* Billions of questions race through my mind. *How do I have a beard in the future? What is future me doing here?* I feel lightheaded. My knees feel weak. The world is spinning, then the world turns black.

Returning to My Childhood

The man is sitting next to me. "Hey kid, sorry I scared you. If there's a weird aftertaste in your mouth, it's the healing potion. How are you feeling, kid?" He asks.

"I'm confused, but good," I reply.

Older Janus smiles as he turns to face me. "Where are we?" I ask.

"Wait, you still don't get it?" Older Janus says.

"Get what?" I respond.

"You're in the world of your childhood self," Older Janus replies.

I look back at him, my eyes widen. "WHAT? Just—just no, I don't even want to think about that old feminine body and those girlish thoughts. Why am I here?"

Older Janus turns to face my swollen, red eyes. He gets to his feet, "When I first met my future me, I wanted to forget that we were ever a little girl. I intended to throw out everything related to femininity and anything possessing the wrong gender's memories and sentiments, sufferings. But when I grew older, I remembered this mind, this universe with young female Janus's ideas and emotions trapped in this world. Then I remember how I attempted to forget about the younger female me—and how this place would soon wither and diminish into nothing more than dust if I allow these memories to fade, that's why everything is overgrown and crumbling in this world currently—"

I draw my legs close to my chest, tucking my face into my lap.

"—because you wanted to forget about your female self when you eventually converted to male and—Janus? Are you all right?" Asks Older Janus

I feel nauseous. My cheeks burn. Hot tears well up in my eyes. I want to kick and scream but I shout instead, "Ju-Jus-Just SHUT UP JANUS! I KNOW IT'S ALL TRUE BUT JUST STOP TALKING ABOUT IT." I see older Janus moving and leaning toward my small, balled-up body. I yell even louder, "GET AWAY FROM ME!"

"Janus," Older Janus scolds. "Breathe and follow me: In on one, two, three, four; hold it, out on one, two, three, four," he repeats himself until I am calm. "Try that next time you feel emotional," he beams at me.

After the mindfulness session, Older Janus helps me to my feet and says, "Follow me, kiddo."

The Murals

Together, Older Janus and I walk through trees surrounding the lawn. As we walk over a worn bridge, I glance over the edge, seeing a raging river rushing beneath. Noticing Older Janus striding away, I hurry back to him. I finally see our destination in the distance: a small wooden cottage decorated with climbing ivy and small flowers.

"Come on, we're almost there," he walks faster, hurrying with excitement.

To the left of the cottage, there is a rock wall with a wooden door. The door, cracked and filthy, has spider webs draping from the stone door frame. Older Janus opens the door.

"Little ones first," he motions with a flourish of his hand.

I enter the space through a room branching into a small shaped tunnel. Tiny windows along the curved edge light the room. A flash of color in the tunnel catches my eye. Walking to the tunnel, I admire the colorful, abstract murals adorning the walls. A blue line lightly covered in a layer of pink fades to only blue with crimson splatters near the blue.

"What are these paintings for?" I ask Older Janus.

Older Janus smiles. "Think about it," Older Janus says.

I roll my eyes. The deeper I walk into the tunnel, the more crimson streaks cover the artwork.

"I have no idea. What do they mean?" Older Janus walks into the tunnel with me, staring ahead while he speaks, "Think of this as a timeline; the pink covering eventually disappears, doesn't it? Just like how you discovered yourself. The red splatters represent your constant eruptions of anger and other feelings you are holding in. Further into the wall, more and more red splatters appear as you keep lashing out at the people you love. This is all because you haven't told anybody about the true trans you." His eyes meet mine.

"But why is it in my female world?" I ask.

"There's the million-dollar question," Older Janus grin widens. "It's here because being female is always a part of you. The process, the life of pretending to be female, is a part of the story that produced the male Janus," says older Janus. "You don't need to forget the other you to come out." He bends down to one knee and places his hand on my shoulder. "You don't have to forget the first you for the true you to come out. You simply must allow yourself to be YOU. I need you to come out of the closet. You're going to tell your parents, 'I'm trans,' okay?" He playfully punches my shoulder, "You got it, just tell them. **What are you waiting for, bud?**"

I nod my head. Saliva builds in the back of my throat. I try not to cry, but I can't hold it back. Tears sting my eyes, streaming down my cheeks. I'm not sure why I'm crying, but I know hearing the truth heals but hurts all at once.

Coming Out of the Closet

We hurry back over the bridge, where the rushing river has become a small creek. Older Janus doesn't even stop to question it. The full moon shines, a spotlight of clarity in the dark night. As Older Janus and I head back through the open fields, I can't help but notice the beauty of this place, a place I once hated with all of my being.

As we walk into the closet and through the wall, the closet shakes and trembles, transporting me back home. I hug Older Janus.

"Thank you." I say, I let go of him and open the closet door. I step into my room feeling transformed. The air feels different—crisper and fresher. Even I feel different: I feel more free and more me.

PART TWO

Affirming the Community

In this section, we provide lessons and stories that reveal and affirm T*GC communities and histories.

Figure P2.1.
The first FTM Pride contingent in the SF Pride Parade of 1993. Reproduced with permission.

CHAPTER SEVEN

Two-Spirit People and the Impact of Colonialism in California

OLIVIA GARRISON

Introduction

As an educator, I have often reflected on the narratives we intentionally or unintentionally create when we design lessons for our students. One area where this is particularly problematic is the Mission Project.[1] The "Mission Project" offers a story that glorifies the era of Spanish settler colonialism, the slavery, exploitation, and mass murder of Indigenous people and the attempted destruction of their cultures. As the California History and Social Science Framework states, "Building missions from sugar cubes or popsicle sticks does not help students understand the period and is offensive to many."[2]

Deborah A. Miranda (2015), an Indigenous poet, professor, and Two-Spirit person, articulated this point when she said,

> It's time for the Mission Fantasy Fairy Tale to end. This story has done more damage to California Indians than any conquistador, any priest, and soldado de cuera (leather-jacket soldier), any smallpox, measles, or influenza virus. This story has not just killed us, it has also taught us to kill ourselves and kill each other with alcohol, domestic violence, horizontal racism, internalized hatred. We have to put an end to it now.

This lesson replaces the Mission Project with a project that uplifts Indigenous voices, focuses on resistance, and centers Indigenous joy through creativity. Students will learn about the diversity of gender and gender expression in California Indigenous communities. They will be confronted with gendercide and genocide. Above all, they will explore how Indigenous people understand gender in the past and today.

Details

Topics/Curricular Connections

- History and Social Studies

Grade Level/Audience

- Grade 4 and up

Learning Objectives

- Define the term Two-Spirit in the context of California history
- Explain how the term Two-Spirit relates to gender and gender diversity
- Engage with various primary source materials
- Interpret the meaning of words and visuals.
- Evaluate the impact of colonialism on Indigenous culture through the lens of gender.
- Explore the lasting impact of colonialism on Two-Spirit people.

Common Core Standards

- CCSS.ELA-LITERACY.RI.4.4, 5.4: Determine the meaning of general academic and domain specific words or phrases in a text relevant to a grade 4 (5) topic or subject area. Integration of Knowledge and Ideas.
- CCSS.ELA-LITERACY.RI.4.7, 5.7: Interpret information presented visually, orally or quantitatively.
- CCSS. ELA-LITERACY.W.4.1, 5.1: Write opinion pieces on topics or texts, supporting a point of view with reasons and information.

CA HSS Framework

- HSS 4.2.5. Describe the daily lives of the people, native and non-native, who occupied the presidios, missions, ranchos, and pueblos.
- "To bring California's history . . . to life . . . and to promote respect and understanding, teachers emphasize its people in all their ethnic, racial, gender, and cultural diversity." (Gr. 4, Ch. 7, p. 68)
- "Missions were sites of conflict, conquest, and forced labor. Students should consider cultural differences, such as gender roles and religious beliefs, in order to better understand the dynamics of Native and Spanish interaction." (Gr. 4, Ch. 7, pp. 76–77)

TWO-SPIRIT PEOPLE

Materials
- Access to the internet and/or library resources for research
- Writing materials (paper, pencils, computers, etc.)

Compelling Questions
- What is being Two-Spirit, and how does it relate to gender?
- How did the missions and settler colonialism impact how Californian Indigenous peoples express gender?
- What was life like for Two-Spirit people before colonization?
- What was life like for Two-Spirit people after colonization?
- How do Two-Spirit people resist colonization today?

> "What comes to mind when I imagine being responsive in trans* and gender creative communities is agency. I currently teach small cohorts of students about social change–to take on a project at our school site and then try to expand from there. Something that's worked in the past is having students, myself, or other presenters come in to have language and education around queer visibility: How do we educate others about our trans* and queer identities to work towards humanizing our communities?
>
> This reimagining is harder than I'd first thought it would be. I think about how I show up in the world when I leave my front door every morning as a trans* person. I am not afraid, but society is afraid of my existence. I am proud of being in touch with my feminine side and my masculine side. To me, acceptance from other people without having to code switch every time I walk into public spaces is the cultural shift that's needed. I'm a human, you need to accept that." – B. Flores

Lesson Steps

Understanding Sex vs. Gender, Introduction to Two-Spirit Communities

Whole Class

- Explain to students that today you will teach them about an essential aspect of Indigenous California culture: Two-Spirit people.
- Review with them the concept of gender vs. sex.
  - Suggested Video Resource: Range of Gender Identities
- Project or write the following onto the board: Biological sex involves our bodies. It involves physical traits we have. But gender depends on how you see yourself. It also depends on how society sees you. It can change based on country and culture.
- Read the statement aloud to the class two times.
- Annotate the statement by defining the words and helping students to understand the meaning of the statement.

- After reading that quotation, have students respond to the following questions on paper, via Google classroom, or even on a post-it note:
  - In our community, what does gender typically look like?
  - What does it look like in your family?
- Ask students to answer with their whole group for the first question about gender in our community. Remind them that you will ask for volunteers to share.
- Have volunteers share.
- Highlight to students that gender roles are cultural. What it means to be a man, woman, or another gendered person can depend on where you live, your religion, and your culture.

Independent[3]

- Students have the option to do one of three things:
  - Watch the video What Does "Two-Spirit" Mean? On YouTube
  - Read the article "Two-Spirit" by The Indian Health Service
  - Listen to the podcast episode Two Spirit People in Native American Cultures from the Unsung History podcast or Two Spirit from the Changing Our Stories podcast.
- Students should answer the following questions on Google classroom or in their notebooks:
  - What does "Two-Spirit" mean? (Pause the video, re-read, or re-listen if you need to)
  - How is being "Two-Spirit" related to gender?
  - What is something you learned about Two-Spirit people that you would like to share with the class?

Deepening Knowledge About Two-Spirit Communities

> "[In school, I wish I had access to an inclusive curriculum] . . . I would love to learn about the AIDS crisis, I would love to learn more about ballroom culture, and I would love to learn about Bayard Rustin and these Black people who were queer in that time and didn't just pop up when everybody had AIDS. That's how they make it seem: that gay people came in the 1970s, and they came with AIDS. That was not the case. I would love to learn more about everyone else that came before that, but also what happened in those moments. I would have loved to learn about that stuff that would, in some way, have helped me with who I am today. I acknowledge my past, I know my past, and now I'm going to continue their fight." – Benjamin

Whole Class

- Give students access to the Student Handouts, which contain reading and primary source material.

TWO-SPIRIT PEOPLE

- Close read the *Background* with the students and model good annotation skills.
- Have students answer the question under the background and share their answers in the class chat.
- Next, work through each *Primary Source* one-by-one:
  - Read the source aloud to students.
  - Have students share difficult vocabulary before proceeding.
  - Then, have the students reread the source silently.
  - Give students ample time to respond to the questions under each source—this can be done in small groups or individually— and review their responses together before proceeding to the next source.
- Read the *Closing Text* aloud to students. Have students share difficult vocabulary before proceeding. Then, have the students reread the source silently.
- Once students have moved through the entire handout, bring them into a whole class discussion to address the following questions:
  - What do you think it was like to be a Two-Spirit during colonialism?
  - How do you think Two-Spirit people stood up for themselves at that time?

Independent

- Have students read the following article, which includes photos of Two-Spirit people. Ask them to share two things they noticed in the pictures when they return to a whole group setting.

Whole Class

- Watch the video Never Not Been a Part of Me together in class.
- Next, discuss the following questions:
  - How have Indigenous Two-Spirit people resisted colonialism today?
  - What are some of the challenges they face today because of colonialism?
  - How do Two-Spirit people thrive today?
  - How can we, as a community, do better to respect the diversity of gender within Native and non-Native communities?

Application of Knowledge

Students have learned about the history of Two-Spirit people, their active resistance, and how they thrive. Students can reflect on those three themes through completion of one of the following activities:

- Government Letter
- Appreciation Art
- Informative Podcast
- Poem/Song

Applying the Three Guiding Frameworks

The Gender Identity Complexities Framework

This lesson centers gender *complexity* by highlighting the histories and contemporary lives of Two-Spirit people, including how Two-Spirit identity has changed over time. Students learn about resistance and advocacy (*critical consciousness*) while unpacking sex, gender, gender roles, gendercide, power, and the importance of culture and social context.

This lesson also asks students to examine the way gender and gender roles play out in their own families and their communities. Offering this learning to students affirms gender complexity, *authenticity*, and the possibility of dynamic *self-definition*.

> "I think Chinese Americans, or Chinese people, in general, they're not usually known for being loud or queer. They're usually known for being quiet, complacent, the model minority. I identify as nonbinary and lesbian, and I'm very proud to be Chinese American. I want to be there to show other Asian Americans, to say that you don't have to be what you're told, to be quiet, or to the norm, or anything that doesn't allow you to be yourself. And my sister, she's also an activist, and she's amazing. She was always there to support me and to show me that it is okay to be me. So that helped me a lot growing up. She helped me a lot to find myself because she's also older than me. So, she knew a lot more. So is my mom, both my parents and my dog, my loud dog, teaching me to be loud." – E. Chen

The Bridge to Thriving Framework

This lesson asks students to examine gender and how culture impacts our expressions of gender in our communities. It affirms that there is no correct way to express gender. The lesson ends with a critical question: How can we, as a *community*, do better to respect the diversity of gender within Native and Non-native communities?

The lesson also offers a model of *resistant identity*, with Indigenous people fiercely rejecting colonial attempts to erase who they are (both in the past and in the present) and finding ways to thrive. By showing Two-Spirit people engaging in *self-determination* and building impactful communities, this experience offers a blueprint for *self-assertion*, as well.

The Historically Responsive Literacy Framework

This activity highlights the contributions of Indigenous LGBTQ+/SGL young people (*identity*) as wise guides for designing thriving. This lesson asks students to *critically* examine the cultural conflict between Western and Indigenous notions of gender, as well as colonial harm and Indigenous resistance, with particular attention to sexual orientation, gender identity, gender expression, race, and age. Students do this by practicing the *skills* of interpretation, analysis, and critical thinking. They ponder significant questions, like "How do Two-Spirit people thrive today?" (*intellect*) Finally, participants will see Two-Spirit people today experiencing *joy* as a means of thriving.

Notes

1. See Graff, 2017.
2. California Department of Education, 2017.
3. This can be done asynchronously, independently, or in small group settings depending on your student and classroom needs.

References

Amaze.org. (2019, June 20). *Range of gender identities* [Video]. YouTube. https://perma.cc/J4N2-AAPQ

California Department of Education. (2017). California: A changing state. In *History social science framework for California public schools: Kindergarten through grade twelve* (pp. 66-94). https://perma.cc/37VZ-XJ6W

Garrison, O. (n.d.). *Student activities: Appreciation art.* https://docs.google.com/document/d/1o6uv9PVj9nVqJODEuMcBlmQITx3aZoIF/edit?usp=drive_link&ouid=100454804064360656722&rtpof=true&sd=true

Garrison, O. (n.d.). *Student activities: Government letter.* https://docs.google.com/document/d/1k2jy5gvLkioDUj1C_SDWSTzcfHzFmVIf/edit?usp=drive_link&ouid=100454804064360656722&rtpof=true&sd=true

Garrison, O. (n.d.). *Student activities: Informative podcast.* https://docs.google.com/document/d/1BZmatt6etld-X0DO4pNjnqx-ofWMK0vY/edit?usp=drive_link&ouid=100454804064360656722&rtpof=true&sd=true

Garrison, O. (n.d.). *Student activities: Poem/song.* https://docs.google.com/document/d/13RBb2tHPOWlejVPKV6kSYd3SruZOo1xx/edit?usp=drive_link

Garrison, O. (n.d.). *Student handouts: Joyas and missionaries.* https://docs.google.com/document/d/1gPm4xCrJzeKFAsTsbRNgGROG61hNCLhW/edit?usp=drive_link&ouid=100454804064360656722&rtpof=true&sd=true

Graff, A. (2017, August 31). *The next generation of California public school students will skip the 'mission project'.* SF Gate. https://www.sfgate.com/news/article/California-public-schools-mission-project-model-11953722.php

Miranda, D. A. (2015). *Lying to children about the California missions and the Indians.* Zinn Education Project. https://perma.cc/57FH-GT4A

Oakland Museum of California. (2019, June 3). *Never not been a part of me* [Video]. YouTube. https://perma.cc/DN2K-GFZ3

Pollock, K. T. (2022, June 20). Two-Spirit people in Native American cultures [Audio podcast episode]. In *Unsung History Podcast.* https://perma.cc/FLM7-EFSR

Smardo, A., & Benally, M. (2018, February 28). Two-Spirit [Audio podcast episode]. In *Changing Our Stories.* https://perma.cc/C7EA-QD4L

Swan-Perkins, S. W. (2018, November 20). *5 Two-Spirit heroes who paved the way for today's LGBTQ+ community.* https://www.kqed.org/arts/13845330/5-two-spirit-heroes-who-paved-the-way-for-todays-native-lgbtq-community

Them. (2018, December 11). What does "Two-Spirit" mean? [Web series episode]. *InQueery*. YouTube. https://perma.cc/575R-HRXM

U.S. Department of Health and Human Services. (n.d.) *Two Spirit*. Indian Health Services. https://www.ihs.gov/lgbt/health/twospirit/

INTERLUDE THREE

"*I am currently in a performing arts school . . . Crazy enough, there is a gender-neutral bathroom. I see people that are like me, and it kind of helps me feel like I belong somewhere. It really kind of helps me feel like I can be myself with my identity and my friends. It makes me feel safe, even being nonbinary, it doesn't make any difference.*

[Cathery]: There were a lot of complexities in the city we were living in while in California. [When El] went to bathrooms that matched their assigned birth sex, [it was hard] at times.

[El]: I was pushed out or I was questioned at the door by this group of five-year-olds, and I'm a fifth grader, and I'm standing there being questioned by five-year-olds so it's really odd.

[Cathery]: So, for a long time, El didn't want to go to the bathroom by themselves. If we were outside somewhere, or we were in a school, one of us would always go with El, because El was scared of the type of verbal and physical reactions, people would have to El because they only think of gender in a binary way. So, when we moved, knowing that we were moving to Texas, and the anti-LBTQIA bills in that state, we were very intentional about finding a gender affirming school. So, El is actually at a real public school, because we're public school people, but leadership matters . . .

So, some of the things that El is naming now about having places to change, having pride flags at school, or people calling each other out when they're not using their pronouns, having nonbinary teachers, it's because the leadership of the school and district have made that intentional, and also, it's an act of resistance to the broader politics of this state. I want to frame that because it's not by luck. There are pockets of resistance everywhere." – E. Chen & C. Yeh

CHAPTER EIGHT

Female Husbands

JADA THOMPSON, JAY WANG, AND CAROL JACOB

> "When I think about my school experiences through the lens of my gender identity/ expression, what I needed from schools and the people who impacted my education in order to be affirmed, feel celebrated, and get my needs met was simple: any acknowledgment that trans* and gender-creative people existed. It would have helped contextualize my quiet struggle by giving me some kind of framework to understand myself.
>
> Nowhere in my history or social studies classes, nowhere in biology or music, art, or health classes was there any mention of any trans* or gender creative person's contribution, much less existence. I never met any representation that spoke to me, or mirrored me, until advanced level English when we learned about Oscar Wilde and cross-dressing male actors in Shakespeare and ancient Greece. Even then, these artists were presented mainly as anomalies, oddities, or as an example of something less advanced people did in the past.
>
> What getting my needs met could have looked like was inclusion of trans* and gender creative artists, scientists, and cultural creatives into the general curriculum, music and theater departments using gender-blind casting for their shows, and having a special office with a trained counselor for the budding trans* or gender creative child to enjoy a safe and supportive space within the school environment.
>
> It could have looked like gender non-specific bathrooms and multi-gendered locker rooms with private, individual changing areas like some European bathhouses.
>
> It could have looked like classroom projects that encourage all students to think about gender and how ignorant assumptions around it limit everyone's experience as a human being. It could have meant learning that intersex people are a biological truth that needs no correction, and that gender creativity itself exists as a fundamental truth about humanity - and always has." – K. James

Introduction

THIS LESSON RAISES AWARENESS about the existence of female husbands and engages students in meaningful conversations about gender and gender roles in society. Through a variety of activities and resources, including listening to a podcast, participating in discussions, peer-teaching, and conducting individual research, students will have the opportunity to explore key concepts related to gender and gender roles and learn about historical figures mentioned in the podcast. We hope this lesson will be an engaging and thought-provoking experience for students.

Details

Topics/Curricular Connections

- Social Studies

Grade Level/Audience

- Grade 9 and up

Learning Objectives

Students/participants will:

- Become aware of the existence of female husbands
- Engage in meaningful conversations about gender and gender roles in society
- Become familiar with historical figures discussed in the core text
- Use real world topics to practice critical thinking and problem solving

Common Core Standards

- RI.9-10.1: Cite strong and thorough textual evidence to support analysis of what the text says explicitly as well as inferences drawn from the text.
- RH.9-10, 11-12.2: Determine the central ideas or information of a primary or secondary source; provide an accurate summary that makes clear the relationships among the key details and ideas.
- RH.11-12.4: Determine the meaning of words and phrases as they are used in a text, including analyzing how an author uses and refines the meaning of a key term over the course of a text (e.g., how Madison defines faction in Federalist No. 10).
- WHST.9-10.7, 11-12.7: Conduct short as well as more sustained research projects to answer a question (including a self-generated question) or solve a problem; narrow or broaden the inquiry when appropriate; synthesize multiple sources on the subject, demonstrating understanding of the subject under investigation.
- WHST.11-12.8: Gather relevant information from multiple authoritative print and digital sources, using advanced searches effectively; assess the strengths and limitations of each source in terms of the specific task, purpose, and audience;

integrate information into the text selectively to maintain the flow of ideas, avoiding plagiarism and overreliance on any one source and following a standard format for citation.

Materials

- Podcast transcript handouts or digital files
- Writing tools
- Worksheet
- A Jamboard could be a great tool for presenting this lesson's questions and capturing students' thinking along the way.

Compelling Questions

- What does learning about the histories and experiences of female husbands reveal to us about how society constructs gender and gender roles?

Lesson Duration

- Likely 3–5 hours

> *"Access is the first thing that comes to mind with affirmation. Specifically, around bathrooms, or in things like overnight camping, appropriate housing. If housing is done by gender, are there opportunities for either mixed-gendered housing or housing that has no gender so that anyone can be comfortable there? But for affirmation, in order to have access, to create those spaces, you have to affirm that we exist in the first place. And so, it would serve as a representation of just being able to see that that is an option, maybe even before I know that it's the option that I need, would give me the affirmation to maybe explore my identity or the confidence to actually use the bathroom that I know is right for me.*
>
> *Affirmation and acknowledgment that we exist would have to come first, and then, actually believing us when we say the things that we say, whether that be who we are, or what we need. Because we can't create access, or let people feel like they belong somewhere, or meet their needs if we're never asking them what their needs are."* – B. Matthews

Lesson Steps

Engaging Students

- Teachers are encouraged to create a container[1] in the classroom for engaging with this lesson, including establishing norms, attending to accessibility needs, and preparing for dynamic social and emotional considerations that might arise.

- Teachers will begin by inviting students to reflect on the following questions, capturing their responses somewhere the whole group can see:
  - When you think of the word "female," what comes to mind?
  - When you think of the word "husband," what comes to mind?
  - What if we put those words together? What comes to mind when you think about the phrase "female husband"?
  - Now, looking back on each of these concepts—female, husband, and female husband—think about *why* you imagine what you do. Where and how have you learned to understand these concepts?

Exploring Concepts, Skills, and Experiences

- Now that students have activated and reflected on their prior knowledge, they can be introduced to the episode Who Were History's 'Female Husbands?' from the *Getting Curious* podcast hosted by Jonathan Van Ness. In this episode, Van Ness interviews scholar Jen Manion about her book, *Female Husbands: A Trans History*.[2]
- Students will be split into small discussion groups (2–4 students) and given the podcast transcript to read as they listen along. Students can be invited to note their thoughts and reactions as they listen/read. The transcript can be downloaded at the podcast link.
- NOTE: Teachers are encouraged to be attentive to how students are responding, with an eye to teachable moments, tensions, and breakthroughs that might warrant an immediate response.
- Stop at intervals to give discussion groups an opportunity to chew and review[3] together, noting their wows and wonders (you will want to change the worksheet headers to match this lesson). Some suggested time stamps for pausing are listed below with Listening Questions. In addition to answering the Listening Questions, discussion groups can also respond to these prompts at each pause:
  - What surprised or stood out to you in this chunk of the interview? (wows)
  - What ideas, topics, or people do you want to learn more about? (wonders)
  - How did you feel while listening to this section? Why do you think those feelings came up?
  - Suggested podcast chunk pause points:
    - 00:03:49
      - Listening Question: "How are female husbands being described/defined at the start of the episode?"
    - 00:11:31
      - Listening Question: "How does the term 'transing gender' help us define queer history?"

- 00:25:36
    - Listening Question: "How did the female husbands that were mentioned present themselves within the community (work, social status, mannerisms)?"
- 00:34:19
    - Listening Question: "How has the term 'transing gender' and 'transgender' changed over time?"
- 00:42:48
    - Listening Question: "What is the term 'Boston Marriages'? What factors made Boston marriages 'socially acceptable'?"
- (the final interval goes to the end of the podcast)
    - Listening Question: "How has the press/media been helpful throughout history for trans* people? How has the press/media been harmful throughout history for trans* people?"

> "I did not experience anything schools and educators did that worked especially well, because no one said or did anything...
>
> What I believe schools and educators can do is work to create learning environments where all are respected and treated equally, celebrated for their unique qualities, and none are singled out as different, as an 'outsider' to normal.
>
> Schools and educators can create these environments in two ways. First, interrogate themselves and their own learned assumptions about gender they picked up from their schools and society, even going so far as to ask themselves why they identify with the gender identity they do.
>
> Secondly, schools and educators need to take their lessons from the kids themselves. Younger generations already consider unique gender expression a given, a non-issue, just another acceptable vector of teen identity like enjoying video games or horseback riding, or creating music and digital art. One's gender expression is just another piece of the overall person, not something, honestly, in need of writing books about. They don't understand why some people are upset about gender enough to pass laws banning them from safe bathrooms, sports, and hobbies of their choice, and necessary, life-saving medical care.
>
> I live for the day that free expression of gender creativity is the accepted norm for all, where it would be weird for someone NOT to spend at least some time experimenting with their gender expression, their body, or its meaning in the world." – K. James

- Ask groups to come up with a brief summary of their discussion to share with the larger class. One person could write the summary, while another could share it out loud. The summary should report an overview of the group's wows, wonders, what feelings came up, and what the group thinks are one to two key takeaways from the podcast.

- Move to a whole group configuration and:
  - Invite each group to share their discussion summary, then
  - Invite the whole class to review their responses to the first activity and discuss how their thinking has evolved now that they've learned a bit more.
- Invite students to spend 5 min reflecting individually on the following questions, before returning to a whole class discussion:
  - How have the gender roles that we assign to people (i.e., being men and how men are expected to behave or being women and how women are expected to behave) influenced how you view the term "Female Husband"?
  - How can gender roles be hurtful? How can they be helpful?
  - Who benefits from gender roles? Who is harmed?
  - What if there was a term "Male Wife"? Do your answers above change? If so, why?
  - Power dynamics and privilege play a role in our everyday lives. When considering the history of Charles Hamilton and Harry Stokes, how are trans* people susceptible to harm within the context of romantic relationships? How can we work to combat and/or limit this harm?
  - What has learning about this topic revealed to you about how humans construct gender and gender roles?

Elaborating on and Evaluating Learning
- As a culminating activity, ask students to research one gender-diverse person who they are curious about.
  - Examples of gender-diverse folx whom students might research include:
    - The Zuni artist We'wha
    - Activist Miss Major Griffin-Gracy
    - Councilwoman Andrea Jenkins
    - Socialite Lucy Hicks Anderson
    - Landowner Anne Lister
- Students summarize what they have learned about the historical figure in a half- to one-page write-up.
- Students can post their summaries and explore them through a class gallery walk, leaving wows and wonders on sticky notes next to each paper.
- Teachers can also adapt the culminating product to be a blog post, TikTok video, piece of visual art, etc.

> "Do I want to teach something with a queer character? Yeah, that would be great. But at the same time, I could just teach the same old classic stuff and also have these other access points for people where they could still potentially find that connection and find

> *that belonging. I'm a millennial, and grew up in the era of fanfiction, Tumblr, and stuff like that, where we created queer stories where there were none, and that was a big part of queer identity. Even now, I still do the same thing, or kind of rewrite plot points for major cultural stories, like 'what if Jess from Gilmore Girls was a queer girl instead?' That would be amazing, so relatable, and great.*
>
> *When I started teaching, I would say Caitlyn Jenner and Laverne Cox were the two most visible trans women in our culture—and there are lots of weird things that go with those two women being highly visible, and why they're highly visible, and where they're highly visible—but at the end of the day, I had a kid who could ask me about my identity and say, 'like Caitlyn Jenner.' And that was a way that we could understand each other and communicate a point that would have been really hard to communicate otherwise without somebody feeling misunderstood or afraid . . . I think it is really important for some of those main cultural touchstones to be represented for those bigger conversations about transness and queerness because it gives everybody this kind of common vocabulary to talk about it."* – M. Luebbert

Applying the Three Guiding Frameworks

The Gender Identity Complexities Framework

This lesson acknowledges *complex gender identities* by not only showing historical examples of people thriving in their gender complexity around the world, but also by facilitating exploration of the nuances surrounding female husbands and how their existence challenges the gender binary. Students learn about the history of *gender and gender fluidity* across multiple cultures and develop an awareness of how gender-related terms have evolved over time.

The Bridge to Thriving Framework

In this lesson, students are invited to develop increased *critical consciousness* by exploring gender norms and assumptions. Some students may feel affirmed by the recognition that gender diverse people exist, including people who were known as female husbands, and by engaging with the fact that numerous gender variations have existed throughout history and will continue to do so. This could create a sense of *true belonging*.

Studying historical figures who existed beyond and opposed a gender binary offers students concrete examples of *resistant identity* to which they can connect their own experiences. The podcast normalizes the existence and treasures the stories of female husbands and other gender-creative figures, celebrating their refusal to feel small or impossible (*abundance*).

> "As a teacher, people are like, 'We want this to be a safe space.' I'm like, 'No. I know this will not be a safe space.' I'm the token here. I need you to (A) see that I am the token and (B) then be thoughtful about that in listening to me and making time to make space. There are marginalized people who are like, 'I don't want to come to work and teach about racism, I don't wanna come to work and teach about transmisogyny, I don't want to come to work and teach about disability.' As a person who's dripping in privilege in a whole bunch of ways—White, blonde, able-bodied, you name it . . . class, educational privilege, you name it—I feel it's my obligation. And I also know that they probably have not listened to someone like me before. I would like them to realize that and make the time and space to do so.
>
> Last year in grad school, I was writing papers for my advisor about transmisogyny all year long; telling a bunch of these stories plus a whole bunch more. But [it wasn't] until our final group project of the year, when one of the other grad students in my Bank Street leadership class screamed at me that I'm a man, on the Zoom, in front of our groupmates, [that] the professor was actually like, 'Wow. I had listened to you the whole time, but I still didn't quite believe it until I saw it myself.' Which I think is, in some ways, kind of true. It is hard to believe. It's hard to believe any of these things, until you see it for yourself." – A. Daniels

The Historically Responsive Literacy Framework

This lesson is responsive to and encourages literacy around the histories of trans* and gender-creative people. Students practice *criticality* by engaging with questions of power, equity, and oppression in the lives of historical gender diverse communities.

Notes

1. See, also, Block, 2015
2. Please note that the podcast contains profanity.
3. Hammond, 2015

References

Alber, R. (2016, December 06). *Enliven class discussions with gallery walks*. Edutopia. https://www.edutopia.org/blog/enliven-class-discussion-with-gallery-walks-rebecca-alber

Block, J. (2015, January 12). *Educate to liberate: Build an anti-racist classroom*. Edutopia. https://www.edutopia.org/blog/build-an-anti-racist-classroom-joshua-block

Gonzalez, A. (2023). *Creating a safe container for students with community agreements*. Mindful Schools. https://www.mindfulschools.org/inspiration/creating-a-safe-container-student-community-agreements/

Google. (n.d.). *Jamboard*. https://jamboard.google.com/

Hammond, Z. (2015). *Culturally responsive teaching and the brain: Promoting authentic engagement and rigor among culturally and linguistically diverse students*. Corwin.

Kennedy, B. C., & Rosado-Torres, A. (2023). *Wow, worry, wonder rubric.* https://docs.google.com/document/d/1k-JvM9Oiv5SaF45Whqd4MZAf7E9ER3Tr/edit?usp=drive_link&ouid=100454804064360656722&rtpof=true&sd=true

Manion, J. (2021). *Female husbands: A trans history.* Cambridge University Press.

Summers, C. (2023, January 25). *Chunk & chew: Giving learners processing time.* https://leadinglearningmatters.com/chunk-chew-giving-learners-processing-time/

Thompson, J., Wang, J., & Jacob, C. (2023). *Female husbands student worksheet.* https://docs.google.com/document/d/1wvEHio8sRUjdqQqyGp3nbx9uw2ri6eZz/edit?usp=drive_link

Van Ness, J. (Host). (2022, April 27). Who were history's "female husbands"? with Professor Jen Manion [Audio podcast episode]. In *Getting Curious.* https://jonathanvanness.com/podcast/getting-curious-who-were-historys-female-husbands-with-professor-jen-manion/

INTERLUDE FOUR

"When I graduated right at the height of the recession, I had wanted to be a teacher. My parents really [discouraged that, but], yeah, I went and did it anyway. I transitioned at the end of my second into my third year teaching at the social justice school, and kids were like, 'Oh wait! Boys can wear nail polish?' And I was like, 'Yeah, sure, of course!' And then kids copied me. And I had a couple of trans* kids follow me out.

Even at the social justice school, everyone's first response to me telling them I was trans* was to ask about surgery. 'Does our insurance cover the surgery?' 'Are you gonna transition fully?' My co-homeroom teacher, who was also one of our activism teachers, literally asked, 'Are you gonna fly to Thailand and cut your dick off?' I spent 5 more years there post-transition. I had a bunch of kids follow me. I've dealt with constant misgendering, microaggressions, macro aggressions. I had a fifth grader's grandfather grab my boobs, while we sang 'We Shall Overcome' during a school assembly. I was on the Board of Trustees while doing it. I couldn't be doing all the things I'm doing if I weren't dripping in privilege. It's also why I feel obligated to use my body as a wedge, trying to make space.

The most complicated ones are the ways where I'm seen as dangerous to kids by being me, which comes constantly. Like, on field trips, there were times when adults would come up to my kids while we were in public and say 'Hey, do you know your teacher's a man?' and stuff like that. After one of the worst ones, I had to really push my boss for us to have a community meeting afterwards, as a debrief, and kids were bringing up examples from years before that I had never even noticed. . . .

I try because I've been called a groomer, and I've been called a pedophile and been called a 'this,' called a 'that,' you name it . . .

The fact that I am so visible and have a choice about it has helped probably 50 or 60 kids at this point. The first adult they've told they were queer or trans* was me. And it's so much harder for my kids who are multiply-marginalized. There is so much space for my assigned-female-at-birth kids to explore in the middle. There's more space for my white kids to explore and figure things out and try things on and not be seen as a problem." – A. Daniels

CHAPTER NINE

Queering Counter-Narratives

BENJAMIN C. KENNEDY AND ALEX ROSADO-TORRES

Introduction

THE 1969 STONEWALL RIOTS are a clear entry point for students to learn about transgender and queer history in the United States. However, this is not the beginning or the end of transgender liberation work. Transgender people have existed and thrived in cultures worldwide since time immemorial. For one tangible example, please refer to the lesson in this book entitled "Two-Spirit People and the Impact of Colonialism in California." Therefore, we use the words "trans" and "transgender" interchangeably throughout this lesson, understanding that these are contemporary umbrella terms encompassing an expansive community with varied and complex gender identities.

This lesson centers on transgender history and the lived experiences of our community. The knowledge has been created for you, and the primary sources have been compiled; however, you could plug in any population for this lesson on counter-narratives. In addition, some helpful resources for your learning—perhaps useful for preparing to teach this lesson—are shared under resources.[1]

Details

Topics/Curricular Connections
- History/Social Studies

Grade Level/Audience
- Grade 9 and up

Learning Objectives

- Students will be able to critically analyze (trans*) history [*Historically Responsive Literacy, Gender Identity Complexity* Awareness/Affirmation]
- Students will engage with multimodal primary sources and develop cross- and digital-literacies [*Historically Responsive Literacy*]
- Students will engage in deep self-reflection, develop their counter-narratives, and grow confidence to claim these narratives [*Bridge to Thriving*]

Common Core Standards

- CCS.RI.9-10.1-3: Learners can identify the different ways to search for key ideas and meanings in informational texts by identifying thorough, and fact based, textual support.
- CCS.RI.9-10.6: Learners will be able to cite textual evidence to highlight the different ways an author's point of view and/or purpose is explored through rhetoric.
- CCS.RI.9-10.7-9: Learners will be able to explore a diversity of sources to assess and evaluate the arguments made within a source and explore how sources connect, or not, to one another.
- CCS.W.9-10.3: Learners will be able to write narratives using a variety of rhetorical techniques and drawing inspiration from the sources explored.
- CCS.W.9-10.4-6: Learners will be able to engage in the whole writing process by revising and editing their writing through feedback from teachers and peers. They will explore the different ways that writing can be presented and shared.

Materials

- Padlet, Jamboard, or an alternative collaborative creation space
- Transgender History Knowledge Check (can be turned into Google Form)
- Analyzing Primary Sources: Teacher's Guide
- Analyzing Primary Sources: Blank
- Wow, Worry, Wonder Rubric
- Primary Source Examples Handout

Compelling Questions

- How do we interrogate history to identify counter-narratives?
- What steps should we take to analyze multimodal primary sources critically?
- Why is perspective a critical consideration when studying history (primary sources)?
- What can we learn from analyzing and searching for the perspectives of those missing from dominant historical narratives (how to identify counter-narratives)?

Supporting Questions

- What is the relationship between trans* history and counter-narratives?
  - *How do we create and claim our stories and (counter)narratives?*
  - *What "counts" as trans* history, and who "gets" to tell these stories?*
- How have the priorities of the trans* community shifted (or not) since 1969/Stonewall?
- How and why might our personal histories be relevant in the broader studying of history?

Lesson Duration

Synchronous learning can last approximately three class periods, and asynchronous learning can last 2 hours or so.

Lesson Steps

Engaging Students

Asynchronous

- In assigned groups, students will complete a homework/pre-work assignment.
- First, students will create a free account on Padlet, Jamboard, or an alternative collaborative creation space.
- Then, groups will develop a timeline of transgender history based only on their current knowledge without using outside sources.
- Additionally, students will independently complete a transgender history knowledge check. Please make a copy of the knowledge check for your class. The educator will use these to assess students' prior knowledge and set the stage for Exploring Concepts, Skills, and Experiences below.

Synchronous (Day 1, in class)

Using their collaborative timelines and the quiz results as a discussion tool, prompt students with a quick independent write asking what they know about LGBTQ+ history and how they feel about how it is represented/portrayed. Offer this as an anonymous quick write, with the invitation to share aloud with the class to prompt discussion.

Formative Assessment

Results of LGBTQ+ history knowledge check and relative accuracy of group timelines

---

"When I think about celebrating community, I think about how far we've come. (Sharing picture): This is 1993 in San Francisco. This right here is Susan Stryker

> *carrying her daughter. That's David Harrison, who's an actor who was in the Blacklist, played Ivan Stepanov. And, anyway, that's me. With hair. That's Max Valerio. This is Loren Rex Cameron, who published one of the first photography books about trans guys. And this is Stefan Thorne. He was the first San Francisco police officer who transitioned on the job. And then this is Brian Craffey, who's an Anglican priest in Vancouver now, I think. But this was the first time there was ever a trans men's contingent in the San Francisco Pride Parade. So, when I think of a community like this, I think now when I see all the kids connecting to each other on Tik Tok, and people like me connecting to each other on Tik Tok, and I think celebrating community, for me, is about connecting to other people. And it's about the power of hearing your story from someone else's life and how healing that can be to get that support from other people and to have that shared, lived experience." – M. Rice*

Exploring Concepts, Skills, and Experiences

Synchronous (Day 1, in class)

Share the lesson on counter-narratives, outlined in bullets below. Feel empowered to engage with this lesson however feels best, through direct instruction, PowerPoint, a lesson packet, or through some other format. If you need more information, please refer to the resources shared at the end of the lesson.

Review of (or introduction to) primary sources:

- Utilizing the Library of Congress (LOC) definition, primary sources are: "The raw materials of history — original documents and objects created at the time under study. They differ from secondary sources, [which are] accounts that retell, analyze, or interpret events, usually at a distance of time or place."
- This broad definition allows us to understand that many documents and objects count as primary sources. With this in mind, it is crucial to consider how and why particular documents and objects have been preserved while others have not. When analyzing primary (and secondary) source documents, it is critical to:
  – Observe,
  – Reflect, and
  – Question
- These three points are also adopted from the Library of Congress. Teachers can use its Analyzing Primary Sources worksheet as a guide.
- In observing, reflecting, and questioning, teachers can guide students to identify how trans* individuals have so often been excluded from the dominant historical record.
  – We recommend using this blank guide to walk students through understanding the questions they should consider under the ORQ cycle.

Review of (or introduction to) counter-narratives:

- "Counter-narrative refers to the narratives that arise from the vantage point of those historically marginalized. The idea of 'counter-' itself implies a space of resistance against traditional domination."[2]
- How counter-narratives support historically and contemporarily marginalized communities, including queer and trans*, BIPOC, disabled, low-income, and other communities:
  > "The effect of a counter-narrative is to empower and give agency to those communities. By choosing their own words and telling their own stories, members of marginalized communities provide alternative points of view, helping to create complex narratives truly presenting their realities."[3]
- Provide avenues for students to search for potential counter-narratives that may exist in the archives. This lens especially privileges using primary source documents connected to traditionally marginalized people such as the transgender and LGBQIA+ community.
- This analysis of counter-narratives also presents an opportunity for educators to explore the ways other social aspects, such as race, class, ability, education, ethnicity, etc., might also be sought out through a counter-narrative lens.
- Additionally, the concept of counter-narrative can allow traditionally minoritized students to craft their own unique counter-stories. Educators can find more resources in the Mora (2014) article's reference section.

Allow students to independently explore a variety of primary sources from Stonewall that have been compiled and linked in this Primary Source Examples handout.

Then, in small groups, ask students to write their initial responses. Some questions that can help elicit critical responses from students, in addition to the questions from the Observe-Reflect-Question Analyzing Primary Sources handout, include:

1. Question Cluster 1 (Observe):
   a. *What do you notice in or about the documents?*
   b. *What perspective(s) are being centered?*
2. Question Cluster 2 (Reflect):
   a. *Why do you think this document was created?*
   b. *How does this document connect (or not) to our present?*
   c. *What can be learned from analyzing this document?*
3. Question Cluster 3 (Question):
   a. *How does this source connect or relate to other sources of the time?*
   b. *What perspectives might be missing?*
   c. *How might this source be interpreted from different perspectives?*

Finally, ask one student from each group to share their peers' thoughts, inviting more responses and participation as one group's ideas inspire others.

Formative Assessment

Identify how one of these sources might be an example of a counter-narrative. You can use an exit ticket or other format, as appropriate.

Explaining Observations and Findings

Synchronous (Day 2, in class)

In pairs, have students use this Wow, Worry, Wonder Rubric to reflect on and self-assess their work and a partner's work.

Asynchronous

Invite students to find other examples of counter-narratives from trans* history in any format and add to a collaborative space such as Jamboard or Padlet with a brief reflection on:

- Why they chose the example,
- Where they found it, and
- What makes it a counter-narrative?

> "I feel like it can be done in several different ways, and they also correlate to that specific person. We have trans* and gender creative people who are artists, and they make beautiful art, whether they're writing plays, writing poems, drawing, acting, dancing, whatever, they make beautiful things, and they deserve a platform to showcase those things and be celebrated for those things. Beyoncé's album Renaissance, to me, feels very much so like a celebration of Black queer people because we have actually been invited to the table. Not saying that she just used our beats, used our ballroom culture, and jazz, she invited TS Madison, Kevin Aviance, all these people who are icons and invited them to collaborate with her. That is such an excellent example of celebration of our community. But there's just being a nice person, understanding that if they are different from you, that's cool. They still are people, and they deserve love. We deserve care. We deserve everything that you deserve. And showing up as a good solid person is, or can be, one way to celebrate lives. The lives they live, the lives we live." – Benjamin (not the author)

Elaborating on Learning

Synchronous (Day 3, in class)

- Students will create a counter-narrative in groups, choosing from multiple modalities, including infographics, podcasts, videos, graphic novels, etc. - OR -
- Individually create their counter-narrative in any of the listed digital or material modalities
- Refer to the Primary Source Examples Handout for examples.

Evaluating Learning

- Set up a gallery walk for presentations of student-created counter-narratives.
- Peer review/evaluation of gallery walk:
  - Students develop three questions that may linger for each counter-narrative they explore in class. These questions should push peers to think differently about their work while creating opportunities for discussion about the various styles, techniques, and content explored in the course. These questions should be written out, discussed, and shared with the teacher.

Applying the Three Guiding Frameworks

The Gender Identity Complexities Framework

sj Miller reminds us that "those whose gender identities fall outside of the binary tend to be misrecognized and misunderstood, suffering from what we call a recognition gap." Miller notes that "misrecognition subverts the possibility to be made credible, legible, or to be read and/or truly understood."[4] The act of "misrecognition" can be addressed in the classroom by centering historically relevant trans* and gender-creative lives. In centering the real stories of T*GC individuals, educators can address the recognition gap that occurs within dominant systems that have enforced normativity, including schools and classrooms. Additionally, adopting critical literacy skills, which allow students to question issues of power connected to gender, paves the way for using primary and secondary sources identified within this lesson plan. By walking students through the source analysis, they can begin to see themselves and others who may occupy trans* and gender-creative identities, which directly challenges the recognition gap identified by scholars such as Miller.

Schools and classrooms often mirror the societies they are a part of. This claim is substantial because society is still centering normative discourses on gender identity and development. Yet, gender identity is far more complex than many of us have been led to believe. This lesson plan provides myriad examples of the ways gender identity is complex, and centers trans* and gender-diverse perspectives from different points of our collective history to affirm the gender complexity that has always existed.

The Bridge to Thriving Framework

One of the significant components of the *Bridge to Thriving Framework* is exploring what "thriving" looks like within systems and encounters of oppression. Throughout this lesson plan, we present students with genuine trans* & queer individuals who have endured oppression. We also explore the myriad ways that these individuals responded to their oppressions. In centering the activism formulated in response to the oppression experienced by trans* & queer activists of the past, students can see how community paves the way for alternative realities where abundance and relief are prioritized. For example, exploring the legacy of STAR, educators can highlight how resource allocation and distribution were central to fighting oppression. What becomes apparent through critical analysis is that while organizations like STAR were important for selfhood and identity development, they were also crucial to overall community well-being. STAR is a strong example of how individuals came together to go beyond surviving and work toward thriving in community. By focusing on how trans* & queer people have thrived throughout history, educators can create avenues for thinking about what "thriving" looks like in the 21st century. How might an organization such as STAR look today? What would "thriving" look like today vs. the 20th century?

The Historically Responsive Literacy Framework

Muhammad (2020) offers four tenets of historically responsive literacy: identity development, intellectualism, criticality, and building skill. Through this lesson plan, students explore identity development through a diverse range of sources that reflect the communities we hope to learn more about. Learners are also able to embark on new intellectual journeys that present alternative academic knowledge through the varied exploration of primary and secondary sources connected to the Transgender Rights Movement. This is especially important as these forms of intellectualism have often been disregarded by our U.S. school system. Additionally, through the centering of primary and secondary sources connected to trans* and gender-diverse people in our history, students explore literacy as a means to achieve criticality—to question and think about how injustice has been maintained and the ways it has been and continues to be challenged. Students develop their own counter-narratives building literacy as a skill. Finally, through the critical analysis of primary and secondary sources, students explore the different methods and styles people use to develop arguments and pieces of written work.

Notes

1. For additional learning, see Solorzano & Yosso, 2022; Stachowiak & Gano, 2020; and Williamsen, 2021
2. Mora, 2014, p. 1
3. ibid.
4. Miller, 2019, p. 4

References

Alber, R. (2016, December 06). *Enliven class discussions with gallery walks*. Edutopia. https://www.edutopia.org/blog/enliven-class-discussion-with-gallery-walks-rebecca-alber

Barbour, B. (2019, August 29). *The power of short writing assignments*. Edutopia. https://www.edutopia.org/article/power-short-writing-assignments

Center for Teaching Excellence. (n.d.). *Implementing group work in the classroom*. University of Waterloo. https://uwaterloo.ca/centre-for-teaching-excellence/catalogs/tip-sheets/implementing-group-work-classroom

Google. (n.d.). *Jamboard*. https://jamboard.google.com/

Kennedy, B. C., & Rosado-Torres, A. (2023). *Primary source examples handout*. https://docs.google.com/document/d/1i4E1I689rRPyIHZc0_sSX8fMBKU854KvcLchRoXUADk/edit?usp=drive_link

Kennedy, B. C., & Rosado-Torres, A. (2023). *Transgender history knowledge check handout*. https://docs.google.com/document/d/150dFVq1BjEaeFR8lDMZJW_TbenmQWxpFs1qjClVfbiU/edit?usp=drive_link

Kennedy, B. C., & Rosado-Torres, A. (2023). *Wow, worry, wonder handout*. https://docs.google.com/document/d/1k-JvM9Oiv5SaF45Whqd4MZAf7E9ER3Tr/edit?usp=drive_link&ouid=100454804064360656722&rtpof=true&sd=true

Library of Congress. (n.d.). *Primary sources analysis tool*. https://drive.google.com/file/d/1byZAkWkxE6ZmYl4zYAXRgDzXk8XZ_e5U/view?usp=drive_link

Library of Congress. (n.d.). *Teacher's guide: Analyzing primary sources*. https://drive.google.com/file/d/1bpbpE8e8_0VrN3QOUigJIPaa5MBK913D/view?usp=drive_link

Library of Congress. (n.d.). *Using the Library of Congress online: A guide for middle and high school students: Primary sources*. https://guides.loc.gov/student-resources/primary-sources

Main, P. (2022, October 21). *Exit tickets*. https://www.structural-learning.com/post/exit-tickets

Miller, sj. (2019). *Teaching, affirming, and recognizing trans* and gender creative youth: A queer literacy framework*. Palgrave Macmillan UK.

Mora, R. A. (2014). Counter-narrative. *Key Concepts in Intercultural Dialogue, 36*, 1. https://centerforinterculturaldialogue.files.wordpress.com/2014/10/key-concept-counter-narrative.pdf

Muhammad, G. (2020). *Cultivating genius: An equity framework for culturally and historically responsive literacy*. Scholastic Incorporated.

Padlet.com (n.d.). *Padlet*. https://padlet.com/

Solorzano, D. G., & Yosso, T. J. (2002). Critical race methodology: Counter-storytelling as an analytical framework for education. *Qualitative Inquiry, 8*(1), 23–44.

Stachowiak, D.M., & Gano, B. (2020). Understanding transgender oppression in higher education using counternarratives. In: R. Papa (Ed.), *Handbook on promoting social justice in education*. Springer Cham. https://doi.org/10.1007/978-3-319-74078-2_51-1

Williamsen, M. (2021). *How to analyze a primary source*. Carleton College Department of History. https://www.carleton.edu/history/resources/history-study-guides/primary/

CHAPTER TEN

Yassifying Math With "The Hips on the Drag Queen"

EL CHEN WITH CATHERY YEH AND B. E. WAID

About the Author

THIS LESSON WAS CREATED as a collaborative project between me (El), my mother (Cathery Yeh), and a family friend (B. E. Waid). I took the lead. Our goal was to center youth interests, passions, and hopes. We read the call for lesson submission and the frameworks for lesson design together, then we discussed what thriving would mean for me. We talked about what I thought schools would look like if they valued children's authentic selves.

From my perspective, schools should have safety at the foundation and, more specifically, safe spaces for children to be their authentic selves, from gender-neutral bathrooms, to honoring pronouns and nonbinary identities, to being able to see themselves represented in the curriculum, to having allies that push for rights beyond their own.

Improving school safety also means improving inclusion. I wanted to create a math lesson highlighting drag queens because they are inspirational, bold, creative, and joyful. Drag queens refuse hypermasculinity and don't conform to cisgender heteronormativity, but you rarely see them in schools. Instead, you see children teasing each other in the playground using gender slurs as insults. Being "a girl" or being "gay" are used as words of shame. In addition, I intentionally wanted to incorporate drag queens in a mathematics lesson. I felt it was important that inclusion of LGBTQIA+/SGL identities in lessons shouldn't just be when the topic is about gender or sexual orientation. Who gets included in everyday lessons in math, science, and social studies matters.

> "When I imagine celebrating trans* and gender-creative communities, it looks a lot like some Pride events I have attended, where a safe and welcoming atmosphere is generated that supports all attendees being their fully expressed selves—without shame, judgment, or threat to their person. It is the gift of space and time to reflect in joy and be reflected. It is zero need to hide.
>
> Celebrating also looks like finding ways to foreground the unique value and contributions of gender-creative/trans* perspectives, experiences, and voices—those cis-people don't and can't have—both in the curriculum and the classroom. It means talking about important trans* and gender-creative people in history who made a difference.
>
> It means finding ways to fight back against the assumption that trans* and gender creative folx are somehow 'others' whose stories and lives don't matter to the overall human populace, or that we are people who don't matter in politics, art, discourse, or society at large and are therefore disposable, silence-able." – K. James

Introduction

This multi-day experience uses the children's book *The Hips on the Drag Queen Go Swish, Swish, Swish* by Lil Miss Hot Mess, which aligns to the song "The Wheels on the Bus." There are numerous ways to use this book for rich learning in K-2 classrooms, including singing, clapping, and dancing along; noticing colors; noticing shapes; and paying attention to the artist's choices, like showing houses in gray that become colorful as the drag queens march past. Here, we focus on counting.

Details

Topics/Curricular Connections

- Math, Reading/Language Arts, Music, Joyful Movement

Grade Level/Audience

- Transitional/Pre-Kindergarten and up

Common Core Standards

- K.CC.2: Count forward beginning from a given number within the known sequence (instead of having to begin at 1)
- K.CC.4b: Understand that the last number name said tells the number of objects counted. The number of objects is the same regardless of their arrangement or the order in which they were counted.
- K.CC.5: Count to answer "how many?" questions about as many as 20 things arranged in a line, a rectangular array, or a circle, or as many as 10 things in a scattered configuration; given a number from 1–20, count out that many objects.
- K.CC.6: Identify whether the number of objects in one group is greater than, less

YASSIFYING MATH WITH "THE HIPS ON THE DRAG QUEEN" 121

than, or equal to the number of objects in another group, e.g., by using matching and counting strategies.
- K.OA.3: Decompose numbers less than or equal to 10 into pairs in more than one way, e.g., by using objects or drawings, and record each decomposition by a drawing or equation (e.g., 5 = 2 + 3 and 5 = 4 + 1).
- K.MD.3: Classify objects into given categories; count the numbers of objects in each category and sort the categories by count.
- 1.OA.3: Apply properties of operations as strategies to add and subtract.
- 1.OA.5: Relate counting to addition and subtraction.

Materials

- Picture book *The Hips on the Drag Queen Go Swish, Swish, Swish* by Lil Miss Hot Mess
- Unifix cubes (or comparable manipulatives)
- Something to play music on (and perhaps speakers)
- Technology for projecting/viewing large images, as needed

Compelling Questions

- How do we count by 3s?

Lesson Duration

- 2 to 5 days

Pedagogical Notes

- See, Think, Wonder is a thinking routine that supports observation and interpretation. A similar routine is Notice and Wonder. See, Think, Wonder asks students to move through three key questions: (1) What do you see? (2) What do you think about that? (3) What does it make you wonder?
- **Yassifying:** The term "yas" was used widely in the 1980s among queer people of color as an exclamation of excitement and joy and even further back, in the 1890s within the drag ball scene.[1] Yassifying is "the process of making something substantially better than its original version" or "the act of making someone or something gayer" (Urban Dictionary). *The Hips on the Drag Queen Go Swish, Swish, Swish* is a yassified version of the classic nursery rhyme *Wheels on the Bus*, and this lesson is yassifying math exploration.

Lesson Steps

Engaging Students

- Start with the song!

- Ask:
  - Does anyone know the song "The Wheels on the Bus"?
  - What do you think about when you think of the song?
  - Has anyone here ever been on a bus?
  - What did you notice about being on the bus?
- Listen and move:
  - Play the song and invite students to dance, sing, or clap along.
- Explain what to expect:
  - Share that you will be reading a story that is similar to the song, using the same melody and rhythm, but different words and characters!
  - You will use the book to have fun with counting.
  - You want students to pay attention to what they notice, what they think, and what they wonder.
  - Model the processes and routines a few times, so students understand how to participate successfully.

Exploring Concepts, Skills, and Experiences

- Make sure that all students will be able to access the lesson. This might mean using a projector to blow the book pages up big or even an amplifying device towards the back of your classroom.
- Introduce students to the concept of "drag queens." There is a brief description at the beginning of Lil Miss Hot Mess' read-aloud video.
- Familiarize students with the book: Read the book aloud, stopping on specific pages to move students through the See, Think, Wonder routine. The teacher can begin with student-generated observations, thoughts, and questions, then invite them to notice specific things, asking, for example:
  - How many drag queen characters did you notice on this page? Let's count them together.
  - How many different ways of being a drag queen do we see on this page? What do you notice?
- Introduce or review counting to 3, 6, 9, and 12. Teachers can use a number line, or any other numerical print posted in the classroom.
- Use the book for counting: Read the book aloud, stopping on a specific page to ask students to count.
  - Pages with clear images that are easy to count include:
    - "swish, swish, swish" (count bodies/outfits/hips)
    - "stomp, stomp, stomp" (count shoes/feet)
    - "blush, blush, blush" (count pairs of eyes)
  - Pages with clear words that are easy to count include:
    - "swish, swish, swish"
    - "stomp, stomp, stomp"

YASSIFYING MATH WITH "THE HIPS ON THE DRAG QUEEN"

- ■ "blush, blush, blush"
- ■ "twirl, twirl, twirl"
- Ask students to use Unifix cubes to represent values they have observed. For example, if using the "up, up, up all through the town" page, the teacher can invite students to count the drag queens (six) and observe their hair colors (light brown, dark brown, blue, and orange), then say, "Use four Unifix colors to get to the number six." A similar process could be used with the "stomp, stomp, stomp" page featuring pairs of shoes.
  - Another counting activity could be to ask students how many drag queens they see on the left side of the page vs. the right side of the page. They could then pick Unifix cubes, use playdough, or choose other items to represent the images they've counted on each side.
- To incorporate movement, students could be invited to "twirl" parts of their bodies (arms, whole bodies, etc.) with the "twirl, twirl, twirl" segment and be asked, "How many times did we twirl?" The teacher can then invite students to take four different colors to create four groups of three to represent the twelve twirls.

Explaining Observations and Findings

- Students can work in pairs and talk to their partners about what they are doing, noticing, and wondering before sharing out loud to the larger group. Students can describe what they watched their partner do during the activity or explain their own thinking out loud.

Elaborating on Learning

- Students can create a classroom "Counting by 3s" book using drawings or cutouts of the people, objects, or shapes they counted in the book. Students could also create a diorama or other art project.
- Students can perform a readers' theater of the text to support comprehension and fluency.
- Noting that the book takes place in San Francisco, students can think about how this book could play out in their own home city (assuming it's not San Francisco).
- A teacher can use this book to count in threes up to the number 12, then work on counting up to 15 the following week.

Evaluating Learning

Summative Assessment and Feedback

- Teachers can ask students:
  - What was your favorite part of the book?

- What is something you would want to tell your family about or share with a friend?
- What's something new that you learned?
• Students can use a Think Pair Share routine here, as well.

Applying the Three Guiding Frameworks

This lesson is created as a collaborative project with a nonbinary lesbian tween (11-year-old's self-identification), their mother, and a queer, demigender (adult) family friend, and with the tween as the lead. Too often, lessons are created *for* youth, and our goal here is to center on their interests, passions, and hopes. Collectively, we read the call for lesson submission and the frameworks for lesson design and asked El what *thriving* would mean for them. What do they hope schools would look like if they were to value children's authentic selves?

There is a misconception that young children are too young to talk about and understand gender and sexuality. We know that this is a lie. Conversations about gender and sexuality happen every day but they center heteronormative, cisgender ideas and norms. We see drag as an imaginative way for young children to explore non-conforming notions of gender and sexuality through play, dance, and joy. Thus, a centering of drag is inherently connected to the dimensions of the *Bridge to Thriving Framework*, as it allows students to experience pleasure and relief in the expansiveness (*abundance*) of gender identity and gender expression, and to authentically explore what their own gender expression could be when allowed to do so in an affirming setting (*selfhood, community, simply being*). Such a lesson is also consistent with Keenan and Hot Mess' (2020) discussion of drag pedagogy, not only because it centers on drag but also allows students to develop "deeper understandings of queer cultures and envision new modes of being together" (i.e., *community*) in ways that work to resist developing the "scripts" about gender and sexuality that Keenan has discussed in other works.

> "Reflecting upon my own experience, it took me a very long time to figure out how to express my identity. Not just in terms of the actual expression—what I wear, what I do, and how I act—but also, what are the words for this? A lot of it had to do with the fact that my narrative does not match very many narratives out there. Even among trans* narratives, it's still very much in the minority. . . . It was this constant exposure, integrating myself into the community that helped me understand what are the words for that, and where does this sit in that realm? Does it still resonate in similar ways? How do I define it? Having someone tell the same story, with different words, helped me to understand how broad that story actually was.
>
> What's so important about affirming space, the reason that it was uncomfortable, is because the world made it uncomfortable. If people had embraced and accepted it as a part of this journey to someone self-recognizing, I think that makes a huge difference.

> *You can see this in minor ways, the people who have a home where they're not judged, or they're accepted for who they are, have an easier time navigating this than those who don't, obviously"* – S. Javitz

The lesson also is connected to Muhammad's *Historically Responsive Literacy* Framework, as well as sj Miller's *Gender Identity Complexities* Framework. First, the lesson is connected to Muhammad's framework because the lesson:

- allows students to explore various representations of gender identity in an age-appropriate manner (*identity*),
- engages students with several representations of counting by three (*skills development and intellect*), and
- centers on a text that presents gender expression as expansive, unique, and personal, rather than adhering to the traditional scripts of gender and gender identity typically taught in PK-16 schooling (*criticality*).

Second, by centering on a text that celebrates and honors the identities, playfulness, and thriving of drag queens, this lesson embodies the overarching goal of Miller's framework—that is, to present *gender identity* as a complex human phenomenon and to ensure that "students' voices and expressions of gender identities [are] heard, affirmed, and recognized."[2] In using *The Hips on the Drag Queen Go Swish, Swish, Swish*, as the core text, this lesson allows students to begin understanding this central idea and focus on a representation of gender that steps outside of the traditional cisnormative heteropatriarchal views that are centered in schools.

Notes

1. Pandell, 2018
2. Miller, 2019, p. 61

References

Hot Mess, L. M. (2020). *The hips on the drag queen go swish, swish, swish*. Hachette Book Group.
Keenan, H., & Hot Mess, L. M. (2020). Drag pedagogy: The playful practice of queer imagination in early childhood. *Curriculum Inquiry, 50*(5), 440–461
Miller, s. (2019). *About gender identity justice in schools and communities*. Teachers College Press.
Pandell, L. (2018, March 22). *How RuPaul's drag race fueled pop culture's dominant slang engine*. Wired Magazine. https://www.wired.com/story/rupauls-drag-race-slang/
Project Zero. (2022). *See, think, wonder*. Harvard Graduate School of Education. https://pz.harvard.edu/resources/see-think-wonder
Teach For Life. (2018, September 20). *Think pair share*. https://www.youtube.com/watch?v=Mig4olzUy4M
Withers, A. (2023). *Routines for mathematical thinking & engagement*. Math for All. https://mathforall.edc.org/routines-for-mathematical-thinking-engagement/
WNET Education. (2021, August 20). The hips on the drag queen go swish, swish, swish by Lil Miss Hot Mess [Web episode]. *Let's Learn*. https://www.youtube.com/watch?v=k9PJd-kj_6k

CHAPTER ELEVEN

2SLGBTQIA+ Community Centers: A Beacon of Hope

B. E. Waid and Tyrone Martinez-Black

Introduction

WE ARE WRITING THIS chapter in the midst of widespread upheaval: the COVID-19 pandemic is killing and disabling millions while disproportionately impacting students who are Black, Indigenous, and people of color (BIPOC), 2SLGBTQIA+, and who have disabilities; Critical Race Theory (CRT) bans have been levied to eliminate discussion of race and racism in schools; violent assaults and murders of non-binary and transgender people (mostly Black and Latiné) rise every year; and we are seeing record numbers of legislative attacks against the teaching of 2SLGBTQIA+ educational content as well as, against transgender youth themselves.

Young people are being asked to learn academically while being bombarded by threats to their physical health, mental health, freedom, histories, stories, and identities. Years of research have established that developing a positive mathematical identity requires that educators also attend to racial, gendered, sexual, and other identities, and how they are intersectional.[1] Despite this, the mathematics community still struggles to center the voices of our most marginalized students. Students need protective environments that support their safety and, therefore, their readiness to learn.

The many issues listed above have negatively impacted the social and emotional health of BIPOC and 2SLGBTQIA+ students,[2,3] which undermines their ability to thrive.[4] The work of surviving takes up so much of their cognitive energy that it becomes extremely difficult to learn academically.[5] It is imperative to create environments in which "2SLGBTQIA+ and BIPOC students can shift their cognitive focus from simply surviving" and instead turn to thriving.[6] The lesson below makes use of *Transformative Social Emotional Learning*,[7] the *Bridge to Thriving* framework, *Historically Responsive Literacy*, and the *Gender Identity Complexities* framework to illustrate a shift toward mathematics in which our historically marginalized, yet most resilient,[8] students can thrive.

Social Emotional Learning

The Collaborative for Academic, Social, and Emotional Learning (CASEL) describes social and emotional learning (SEL) as:

> the process through which all young people and adults acquire and apply the knowledge, skills, and attitudes to develop healthy identities, manage emotions and achieve personal and collective goals, feel and show empathy for others, establish and maintain supportive relationships, and make responsible and caring decisions.
>
> SEL advances educational equity and excellence through authentic school-family-community partnerships to establish learning environments and experiences that feature trusting and collaborative relationships, rigorous and meaningful curriculum and instruction, and ongoing evaluation. SEL can help address various forms of inequity and empower young people and adults to co-create thriving schools and contribute to safe, healthy, and just communities.[9]

CASEL also identifies five core SEL competencies:[10]

1. self-awareness,
2. self-management,
3. social awareness,
4. relationship skills, and
5. responsible decision-making.

We discuss these competencies in relation to the development of a mathematics identity and teaching/learning experiences in the accompanying Video 1: What is the Connection between SEL & Mathematics?

Sometimes SEL is oversimplified as being "good human beings with one another," but addressing CASEL's five competencies without applying antiracist, gender complex, and equity lenses can simply reproduce our society's dominant, oppressive ways of being. For example, a non-critical approach to student self-management could look like expecting students to remain calm and polite while being subjected to oppressive treatment in classrooms. In recognition of this, CASEL has advanced the concept of Transformative SEL, which is:

> aimed at redistributing power to promote social justice through increased engagement in school and civic life. It intentionally points to competencies and highlights

relational and contextual factors that help promote equitable learning environments and foster desirable personal and collective outcomes.[11]

We elaborate on the application of Transformative SEL in mathematical contexts in the accompanying Video 2: What is Transformative SEL?

A Simple Case of Transformative SEL

Several complex social and emotional events can play out for a student during a single educational experience. Here's a brief illustration of what could be activated during a math lesson.

> Imagine a student in a math class that is exploring basic fractions. If the student understands the key numerical facts at play, such as that fractions are numbers unto themselves and can be positioned along a number line, that knowledge could increase their *sense of belonging* in the mathematics classroom. Their *social awareness* might be activated as they think about whether everyone else in class also knows what a fraction is. In *self-awareness*, they may think, "I know that too."
>
> However, division of fractions may challenge their understanding. In *confusion* about the concept and its application, their sense of *belonging* and *identity* as a mathematician may be threatened. They might wonder, "How do I work/learn with peers when they are doing something I can't do?" *Relationship skills* are activated when they consider asking for help with these difficult tasks. Exercising *self-management*, they may persevere, knowing they are still developing mathematically (*growth mindset*). Our learner might ponder how to accept that they don't know enough yet but continue working to learn more and benefit from the effort. Their decision to be a problem-solver and persevere in their learning would be an example of *responsible decision making*.

Cultural contexts shape the learning process—schools as parts of neighborhoods, mathematics as a discipline, representations of successful learners—all are steeped in complex histories and practices that can impose boundaries around who belongs and who does not. If our learner doesn't see themself learning certain skills and sees no evidence that people like them can succeed at such work, their identity can become vulnerable. This is one place where a teacher's approach exerts profound power over whether the student checks in or checks out.

Well-designed teaching can provide opportunities to practice applying knowledge while deliberately engaging young learners in co-constructing their learning environment. Such teaching will give students:

1. Explicit instruction about understanding and applying social and emotional skills,

2. Opportunities to practice SEL skills and competencies that are embedded into academic work (i.e., well-scaffolded class discussions), and
3. A learning environment that models safety, respect, and purpose so that students can invest their whole selves in learning.[12]

We discuss how this can look in the accompanying Video 3: What Might Transformative SEL Look Like in Mathematics?

The lesson below adapts "Making Mathematical Sense of Food Justice," by Davidson and colleagues[13] to:

1. focus on learning about 2SLGBTQIA+ community centers, as "beacons of hope"[14] and to
2. campaign for greater access to these assets statewide.

We invoke an intersectional,[15] assets-based approach, tapping into existing "funds of knowledge"[16] offered by 2SLGBTQIA+ culture and history.

Details

Topics/Curricular Connections

- Math, History, English Language Arts, Health, Civics

Grade Level/Audience

- Grade 9 and up

Learning Objectives

*Students/participants will **come to know** and/or **be able to do** the following:*

- Explain what a "community asset" is
- Explain what it means to have equitable access to a community asset
- Use geometric principles of right triangle trigonometry, circles, area, and population density to develop a mathematical procedure for optimizing equitable access to a community asset.
- Use mathematics to engage in civic action

> "When I think about our community's needs for housing and health care and mental health care, and ... feeling safe in our communities, because we know the police are not looking out for our communities, there are so many things we need.... When I think about things like shelters, great that they exist, but they are often delineated by the sex assigned at birth, and so they're not safe places. So, especially in our community here ... we have a lot of friends experiencing homelessness, and they would rather be out on the streets than be in a shelter because they are so unsafe, and what does that say about

> *the accommodations we are providing that someone would rather be houseless than have access to a bed and food?*
>
> *. . . I go to a gym that has a trans* flag outside, and a Progress Pride flag, and at the beginning of workouts, there's a question of the day we answer before we start our class and we ask folks to share their name and pronouns, and even if it's the same people at every single class, we still do it. What a simple thing to do. And it doesn't out the one trans* person. I think about having businesses that are connected to Pride. I know, there are certain bars that I can go to because I know they have a relationship with Pride, whether that's philanthropic, whether that's training for their staff to not say 'ladies and gentlemen.' Simple, simple things that can be done to make folks feel like their needs are being met."* – B. Kennedy

Materials

- 2SLGBTQIA+ Community Centers: A History Handout
- Shrinking Budgets and Access Handouts Part 1 & Part 2
- Taking Action Handout
- Teacher Resources:
    - Video 1: What is the Connection between SEL & Mathematics?
    - Video 2: What is Transformative SEL?
    - Video 3: What Might Transformative SEL Look Like in Mathematics?
    - Video 5: How Is Transformative SEL Centered in the Lesson?
    - Smith and Stein's five practices Resource 1
    - Smith and Stein's five practices Resource 2
    - Strategies and Struggles
    - The Jigsaw Method
    - Creating a Google Slides Gallery Walk
- Optional:
    - Video 4: How to Use Desmos to Create a Map of 2SLGBTQIA+ Community Centers
    - Reflections on Race and Gender activity from Waid's (2022) Talking about LGBTQ+ identity: A guide for PK-16 educators
    - Intersectional Equity Handout
    - Defining Equity and Equitable Access Handout

Compelling Questions

- What is a community asset?
- What does it mean to have *equitable access* to a community asset?

Lesson Duration

- 3 to 7 days

Pedagogical Notes

- For this lesson, facilitators will divide participants into "home groups" and "expert groups." Each student will be assigned to explore a portion of the content and become an "expert" who will bring their learning back to the "home group." The home group will then use The Jigsaw Method to put all of the pieces of content together and complete assignments.
- We recommend that educators familiarize themselves with foundational ideas and terminology related to 2SLGBTQIA+ identity. Waid (2022) has created a PK-16 educator guide. Begin with the activity "Reflections on Race and Gender: Creating a Shared Understanding" before launching the lesson below.
- This lesson is focused on the state of New Jersey, but teachers may wish to tailor the handout to reflect the locations of 2SLGBTQIA+ community centers in their home state.
- In our New Jersey map, each point represents a different pride center, with an asterisk (*) indicating a location with multiple centers.
- As an adaptation to this activity, groups might be asked to research the locations of community centers and create their own map on Desmos, using Video 4: How to Use Desmos to Create a Map of LGBTQ+ Community Centers[17] as a guide.
- For students needing additional scaffolding to define "equitable access" teachers can provide the Defining Equity and Equitable Access Handout
- As groups work on the "Part 1" handout, we recommend using Smith and Stein's five practices (resource 1):[18] anticipating, monitoring, selecting, sequencing, and connecting (Smith and Stein's five practices are emphasized in boldface font throughout the text of the lesson steps below). Here are some considerations:
  - The Strategies and Struggles handout provides ideas for the practice of *anticipating*.
  - The use of a monitoring chart is recommended while *monitoring*.
  - For *selecting* and *sequencing*, as teachers decide on a predetermined sequence for moving students through the learning experience, Smith and Stein recommend beginning with a common misconception before moving on to the remainder of presentations. Alternatively, a sequence may represent a progression of mathematical ideas (e.g., using the distance formula, then generating a circle, then mapping population density within a given area). It may also connect the limits of using a particular strategy, then showing how it can be resolved using a subsequent approach (e.g., linear distances or circles won't account for overlapping service areas or concentrations of residents). Other suggestions include beginning with a strategy used by the majority of students, then moving to strategies used by a smaller number, or beginning with more concrete strategies before moving to strategies that are more abstract.

- As students self-assess their mathematical approaches, remind them to refer back to the criteria identified in question 5 of their "Part 1" handout, where they developed their definitions of "equitable access."
- In lieu of a *five practices* discussion, students could complete an asynchronous virtual gallery walk to provide peer feedback on group responses to question 6 of the "Part 1" handout, where they identify the location of a new center to increase "equitable access." Peer feedback should be centered on 1) relationship to the given group's definition of equitable access, 2) soundness of the mathematical method developed to determine the location of the new center, and 3) correctness of mathematical procedures employed throughout the utilized methods.
- We have designed this unit so students may create their own assessment criteria throughout, though teacher checks and approval are recommended at certain points. Alternatively, some teachers may wish to create their own assessment criteria to share with students.

Lesson Steps

What Is a Community Asset?

- Facilitators and students organize "home" and "jigsaw" groups in preparation for the activity.
- In home groups, students read the 2SLGBTQIA+ Community Centers: A History handout together.
- Then, students watch their assigned "expert" video and answer the "expert group" questions, individually. After completing the viewing and questions, students discuss their thoughts with their *expert groups*.
- Once *expert group* discussions are complete, students return to their *home groups*, each having watched a different video. Each member will summarize their expert groups' discussions, then the entire home group will answer the "home group" questions together.
- At the close of this portion of the unit, students will have explored what a community asset is.

Equitable Access to Community Assets - Part 1

- Students can work in small groups to answer the questions in the Shrinking Budgets and Access Part 1 handout. (Teachers, feel free to design this however you'd like.)
- Then, to summarize their learning, students can present their strategies (procedures and methods developed using the handout) in the predetermined sequence as the teacher aids students in making connections between the various strategies presented (*Smith and Stein's practice of connecting*).

Equitable Access to Community Assets – Part 2

- Groups (the same as those from Phase 1.2) continue to think about equitable access by working on the Shrinking Budgets and Access Part 2 handout.
- As groups work on the "Part 2" handout, we recommend engaging in another round of Smith and Stein's *five practices*.[19]
- To summarize their learning, students can present their Part 2 handout strategies in the predetermined sequence as the teacher helps them make connections between the various strategies they and their peers present (*connecting*).
- For students needing additional scaffolding to consider how intersectionality might impact their definitions of equitable access, use the Intersectional Equity handout.

Culminating Project

- Students can use the Taking Action handout to select, design, and complete a final project.

Applying the Three Guiding Frameworks

The Gender Identity Complexities Framework

In introducing 2SGLBTQIA+ Community Centers as community assets, this lesson critiques how such centers are represented (or ignored) in popular culture (*principle 6*). It also disrupts compulsory heterosexism and cissexism by centering community assets created by and for 2SLGBTQIA+ peoples (*principle 7*) and celebrates 2SLGBTQIA+ identities (*principle 10*). Additionally, the lesson allows students to construct their own definition of "equitable access," while also requiring them to consider how a 2SLGBTQIA+ community center's lack of intersectional services impacts their definition/understanding of equitable access (*principles 8 and 9*). Here, intersectional services refer to those that are targeted to specific subsets of the 2SLGBTQIA+ community, such as by racial and ethnic identity, disability, and so on. Finally, in their "Taking Action" projects, students create an advocacy plan, arguing to open a new 2SLGBTQIA+ Community Center at their identified location.

The Bridge to Thriving Framework

Collaborative activities like small group project-based learning, jigsaws, five-practices discussions, and gallery walks create opportunities to build *community*. The lesson's focus on community assets provides a framing that centers *abundance, relief*, and *pleasure*, by disrupting the typical narratives found in lessons used to teach mathematics for social justice, which often center community suffering and what is *lacking*. Finally, students are encouraged to embrace their full *selfhood*, considering equitable access through an intersectional lens, rather than a thin slice of their identities (*simply being*) and provided opportunities to express their autonomy through choice (*selfhood*).

> "I met a lot of my friends at [college], who encouraged me and gave me that self-esteem that I lacked just because I went into a predominantly white school. I really stuffed all that stuff down and didn't think I could come out. And once I took over and saw that there were LGBTQ clubs and people that were so supportive and invested in it, that's what kind of helped me come out of my shell and say, hey, [this college] is a safe zone, we see all these Pride stickers, we see these people putting effort, we see all these other LGBTQ students or even basketball players, cheerleaders, dancers, the male cheerleaders, male dancers, you saw the inclusion for sure, all over campus in different areas." – V. Zepeda

The Historically Responsive Literacy Framework

Our lesson allows students to develop mathematical *literacy* by reading and writing the world with mathematics,[20] and through the use of "non-traditional" texts[21] like a state map, videos, and historical readings. Students examine how 2SLGBTQIA+ communities create spaces for collective thriving (even under oppressive conditions) and make sense of their own identities within the context of this lesson, especially as they consider what it might mean to have "equitable access" to community resources (*historically responsive literacy, identity, and criticality*). The texts and lesson activities serve to develop students' mathematical *skills*, as well as their *intellect* as their understanding of sociohistorical/sociopolitical contexts and mathematical argumentation increases.

Constructs of Transformative Social Emotional Learning

CASEL's Constructs of Transformative SEL allow us to view mathematics as both an *activity* people can *do*, and an *identity* people can *express*. Belonging to a community of mathematicians means negotiating dynamic behaviors, interactions, and postures practiced by members of the discipline. We hold that membership should be open to all humans. In Video 5: How Is Transformative SEL Centered in the Lesson?, we note that the lesson deliberately begins with centering the *identities* and community *belonging* of 2SLGBTQIA+ students. This is intended to invite students to pay attention to how math, 2SLGBTQIA+, and geographic identities intersect. *Agency* is activated when students decide how to explore the questions, or create maps, or craft arguments about the centers. Their *curiosity* is provoked as they dig into the purposes, assets, locations, and contexts of 2SLGBTQIA+ centers, as well as how they serve communities. *Collaborative problem solving* is woven throughout—at both small- and whole-group levels.

Conclusion

Blending project-based learning with action research, this lesson seeks to engage students in meaningful problem-solving that reveals the importance of providing safety and support to fellow human beings. It is also intended to invite educators to adopt a posture of collaboration, mutual learning, holistic support, and power-sharing with students. Our hope is that celebrating these local assets will be both affirming and empowering.

Notes

1. cf. Aguirre et al., 2013; Gholson & Martin, 2019; Lambert et al., 2018; Leyva et al., 2019; Murrell, 2007; Waid, 2020; Yeh & Wong, 2019
2. GLSEN, 2021; The Trevor Project, 2022
3. We write, from this point forward, listing these two identity frames separately to recognize their distinct characteristics, while also respecting that many of us (authors included) exist in a blend or intersection of the two.
4. Darling-Hammond, 2022
5. Hammond, 2015; McInerney & McKlindon, 2014; Menakem, 2017; Nelson et al., 2022
6. See Waid, 2021, para 8
7. Jagers et al., 2021
8. cf. Martin, 2009
9. CASEL, n.d.; CASEL, 2019
10. CASEL, n.d.
11. Jagers et al., 2021, para. 9.
12. Aspen Institute National Commission on Social, Emotional, and Academic Development, 2018
13. Davidson et al., 2020
14. Bradbury-Sullivan LGBT Community Center, 2021
15. cf. Crenshaw, 1991
16. cf. Civil, 2017; Gonzalez et al., 2005
17. The chapter contains several clips of a longer recorded conversation available at Martinez-Black & Waid, 2022, modeled after Martinez-Black and Rezvi's (2021) "All We Have Are Questions" mutual interviewing approach.
18. Smith & Stein, 2011
19. Smith & Stein, 2011
20. Gutstein, 2005
21. Waid & Turner, 2021

References

Aguirre, J. M., Mayfield-Ingram, K., & Martin, D. B. (2013). *The impact of identity in k-8 mathematics learning and teaching: Rethinking equity-based practices.* The National Council of Teachers of Mathematics.

Aspen Institute National Commission on Social, Emotional, and Academic Development. (2018). https://www.aspeninstitute.org/programs/national-commission-on-social-emotional-and-academic-development/

Bayard Rustin Center for Social Justice. (n.d.). *Home.* https://www.rustincenter.org

Bradbury-Sullivan LGBT Community Center. (2021, September 2). *How the Bradbury-Sullivan LGBT Community Center is a beacon of hope.* [Video] YouTube. https://www.youtube.com/watch?v=LZKWB_VL0Ac

The Center. (2019, November 4) *The Center story.* [Video]. YouTube. https://www.youtube.com/watch?v=36EmFxbvme8

Civil, M. (2007). Building on community knowledge: An avenue to equity in mathematics education. In N.S. Nasir & P. Cobb (Eds.) *Improving access to mathematics: Diversity and equity in the classroom* (pp. 105–117). Teachers College Press.

Collaborative for Academic, Social and Emotional Learning (CASEL). (n.d.). *Fundamentals of SEL.* https://casel.org/fundamentals-of-sel/what-is-the-casel-framework/#interactive-casel-wheel

Collaborative for Academic, Social and Emotional Learning (CASEL). (2019). *CASEL guide to schoolwide social and emotional learning.* https://schoolguide.casel.org

Collaborative for Academic, Social and Emotional Learning (CASEL). (2020). *CASEL's SEL framework: What are the core competence areas and where are they promoted?* https://casel.s3.us-east-2.amazonaws.com/CASEL-SEL-Framework-11.2020.pdf

Crenshaw, K. (1991). Mapping the margins: Intersectionality, identity politics, and violence against women of color. *Stanford Law Review* 43(6), 1241–1299.

Cult of Pedagogy. (2015, April 15). *The jigsaw method.* https://www.youtube.com/watch?v=euhtXUgBEts

Darling-Hammond, K. (2022, January 20). Dimensions of thriving: Learning from Black LGBTQ+/SGL moments, spaces, and practices. *Nonprofit Quarterly.* https://nonprofitquarterly.org/dimensions-of-thriving-learning-from-black-lgbtq-sgl-moments-spaces-and-practices/

Davidson, J., Greenstein, S., Basu, D., & Davidson, J. (2020). Lesson 8.3: Making mathematical sense of food justice. In R.Q. Berry III, B.M. Conway IV, B.R. Lawyer, & J.W. Staley (Eds.) *High school mathematics lessons to explore, understand, and respond to social injustice* (pp. 226–231). Corwin & National Council of Teachers of Mathematics.

EdTech Throwdown Podcast. (2020, March 13). *Creating a Google Slides gallery walk in Zoom and Google Meet* [Video]. YouTube. https://www.youtube.com/watch?v=XH63YrzduOM

Gholson, M. L., & Martin, D. B. (2019). Blackgirl face: Racialized and gendered performativity in mathematical contexts. *ZDM 51*(3), 391–404.

GLSEN. (2021). *Policy maps.* https://www.glsen.org/policy-maps/.

González, N., Moll, L.C., & Amanti, C. (Eds.). (2005). *Funds of knowledge: Theorizing practices in households, communities, and classrooms.* Routledge.

Greenlee, M. (2019, July 10). *Teaching elementary students to speak the language of mathematics through mathematical discourse* [Conference session]. Conference for the Advancement of Mathematics Teaching, 2019. San Antonio, Texas, United States. https://www.utdanacenter.org/sites/default/files/2019-07/Greenlee_CAMT_Teaching_Elementary_Students.pdf

Gutstein, E. (2005). *Reading and writing the world with mathematics: Toward pedagogy for social justice.* Routledge.

Hammond, Z. (2015). *Culturally responsive teaching and the brain: Promoting authentic engagement and rigor among culturally and linguistically diverse students.* Corwin Press.

Jagers, R. J., Skoog-Hoffman, A., Barthelus, B., & Schlund, J. (2021). Transformative social and emotional learning: In pursuit of educational equity and excellence. *American Educator* (Summer). https://www.aft.org/ae/summer2021/jagers_skoog-hoffman_barthelus_schlund

Lambert, R., Tan, P., Hunt, J., & Candela, A. G. (2018). Rehumanizing the mathematics education of students with disabilities: Critical perspectives on research and practice. *Investigations in Mathematics Learning 10*(3), 129–132.

Leyva, L, Quea, R., Battey, D., Weber, K., & Lopez, D. (2019). Detailing the potentially marginalizing nature of undergraduate mathematics classroom events for minoritized students at intersections of racial and gender identities. In *Proceedings of the 22nd Annual Conference on Research in Undergraduate Mathematics Education*, 377–381.

Martin, D.B. (Ed.). (2009). *Mathematics teaching, learning, and liberation in the lives of Black children.* Routledge.

Martinez-Black, T., & Rezvi, S. K. (2021). All we have are questions. *Mathematics Teacher: Teaching and Learning PK-12 114*(8), 638–640.

McInerney, M., and McKlindon, A. (2014). *Unlocking the door to learning: Trauma-informed classrooms and transformational schools.* Educational Law Center. https://www.elc-pa.org/wp-content/uploads/2015/06/Trauma-Informed-in-Schools-Classrooms-FINAL-December2014-2.pdf

Menakem, R. (2017). *My grandmother's hands: Racialized trauma and the pathways to mending our hearts and bodies.* Central Recovery Press.

Murrell, P. (2007). *Race, culture, and schooling: Identities of achievement in multicultural urban schools.* Erlbaum.

Nelson, K., Peterson, K. McMillin, L., & Clarke, K. (2022). Imperfect and flexible: Using trauma-informed practice to guide instruction, *Libraries and the Academy, 22*(1), 177–197.

San Francisco Unified School District Mathematics Department. (n.d.). *5 practices for orchestrating productive mathematics discussions: Based on the book by Margaret Smith and Mary Kay Stein.* https://www.sfusdmath.org/5-practices-for-orchestrating-productive-math-discussions.html

Smith, M. S., Steele, M. D., & Sherin, M. G. (2020). Monitoring chart. In *The five practices in practice [high school]: Successfully orchestrating mathematics discussions in your high school classroom.* Corwin. https://resources.corwin.com/5practices-highschool/student-resources/charts-and-templates

Smith, M. S., & Stein, M. K. (2011). *5 practices for orchestrating productive mathematics discussions.* National Council of Teachers of Mathematics.

The Queer Mathematics Teacher. (2022, January 29). *How is transformative SEL centered in the lesson?* [Video]. YouTube. https://www.youtube.com/watch?v=Vxn6qeDW0jk

The Queer Mathematics Teacher. (2022, January 19). *How to use Desmos to create a map of LGBTQ+ community centers.* YouTube. https://www.youtube.com/watch?v=P0kA0-Jrpiw

The Queer Mathematics Teacher. (2022, January 29). *Transformative SEL and LGBTQ+ liberatory education* [Video]. YouTube. https://www.youtube.com/watch?v=tEFwwryJIEI

The Queer Mathematics Teacher. (2022, January 29). *What is the connection between SEL and mathematics?* [Video]. YouTube. https://www.youtube.com/watch?v=RrH_MXScy-U

The Queer Mathematics Teacher. (2022, January 29). *What is transformative SEL?* [Video]. The Queer Mathematics Teacher. https://www.youtube.com/watch?v=_AvxNSw9HzU

The Queer Mathematics Teacher. (2022, January 29). *What might transformative SEL look like in mathematics?* [Video]. YouTube. https://www.youtube.com/watch?v=GhiUEdjdxEk

Trevor Project. (2022, January). *Issues impacting LGBTQ youth.* [Presentation Slides]. https://www.thetrevorproject.org/wp-content/uploads/2022/01/TrevorProject_Public1.pdf

Waid, B. E. (2020). Supporting LGBTQ+ students in K-12 mathematics. *Mathematics Teacher: Learning and Teaching PK-12, 113*(11), 874–884.

Waid, B. E. (2021, March 17)). The Equality Act: What math teachers need to know. *Queer Mathematical Musings: Blog of The Queer Mathematics Teacher.* https://www.thequeermathematicsteacher.com/equality-act/the-equality-act-what-math-Teachers-need-to-know/

Waid, B. E. (2022). *Talking about LGBTQ+ identity: A guide for PK-16 educators.* The Queer Mathematics Teacher. https://www.thequeermathematicsteacher.com/talking-about-lgbtq-identity-a-guide-for-pk-16-educators/

Waid, B. E., & Martinez-Black, T. (2023). *2SLGBTQIA+ community centers: A history handout.* https://docs.google.com/document/d/1TF8ASPC8G90tzKevVbIK3NsEHsH1k-73/edit?usp=drive_link&ouid=100454804064360656722&rtpof=true&sd=true

Waid, B. E., & Martinez-Black, T. (2023). *Defining equity and equitable access handout.* https://docs.google.com/document/d/14rmAsW5WFNv_x1Tm1_CB9wjmJbkmQ5-i/edit?usp=drive_link

Waid, B. E., & Martinez-Black, T. (2023). *Intersectional equity handout.* https://docs.google.com/document/d/18e4H9YG447VRh6MqFHxd09noqRwY_gPm/edit?usp=drive_link&ouid=100454804064360656722&rtpof=true&sd=true

Waid, B. E., & Martinez-Black, T. (2023). *Shrinking budgets and access part 1 handout.* https://docs.google.com/document/d/16JN0gGGhtMOq1YmmyPscsPsUrLcz309o/edit?usp=drive_link&ouid=100454804064360656722&rtpof=true&sd=true

Waid, B. E., & Martinez-Black, T. (2023). *Shrinking budgets and access part 2 handout.* https://docs.google.com/document/d/1e95pWboiE1TV3oxfPeHByr_I3-Y0MIxl/edit?usp=drive_link&ouid=100454804064360656722&rtpof=true&sd=true

Waid, B. E., & Martinez-Black, T. (2023). *Student strategies and struggles handout.* https://docs.google.com/document/d/1FJDoUHPzkBLZpncXudgRVGddJhFNmd7t/edit?usp=drive_link

Waid, B. E., & Martinez-Black, T. (2023). *Taking action handout.* https://docs.google.com/document/d/1fUCHver-HBnGM5YY68sNBIxz07F0s8ad/edit?usp=drive_link&ouid=100454804064360656722&rtpof=true&sd=true

Waid, B. E., & Turner, K. H. (2021). Inqu[ee]ry across the curriculum. *English Journal, 110*(3), 82-88.

Yeh, C., & Wong, A. (2019). The co-construction of competence: An activity system perspective for leveraging and strengthening students' language and mathematics competencies. *Teaching for Excellence and Equity in Mathematics, 10*(1), 17–25.

CONCLUSION

The book you have just explored is an act of defiance. Zealots, bigots, and authoritarian elites are fomenting hatred and passing laws every day to smother any support for trans* and gender-creative people. They don't want this book to exist because they don't want us to exist, either.

This text is a testament to their failure. Each chapter is simultaneously a testimonial, a tool, and a test. A testimonial, because each is evidence that trans*-affirming pedagogy is not only possible but real, successfully implemented in classrooms and ready to be deployed in many more. The depth and scope of the lessons contributed by over a dozen contributors from across the United States illustrates the diversity and strength of our community that perseveres despite the ugliness of the attacks against us.

K. Elliott's "Exploring and Reclaiming Home in Our Bodies" and Bre Evans-Santiago's "Brain Chemicals and Kindness" use music, movement, and words to ground students in an affirming process that can be understood physiologically as the reinforcement of positive neurotransmitter and hormonal circuits, and intersubjectively as the feeling of being at home in one's body.

The following lessons extend beyond the present-day body in both space and time. "Who Are You? A Black Queer Journey to Selfhood and Community Freedom" from Danelle Adeniji and DeKeisha Smith excavates the past struggles and potential resistances emerging from the Black Queer diaspora, while Wendy Garay and Bethany Gonzales' lesson on "Annie's Plaid Shirt" moves beyond the body proper to examine how attire allows us to construct our authentic selves. The importance of being recognized in the roles we inhabit, whether on stage or in day-to-day life, is acknowledged by Ana Cornejo's "Be You," a precursor lesson for the book *Melissa*, and by Shaylyn Marks' "Exploring Identity and Selfhood," which accompanies *All Boys Aren't Blue*.

El Chen provides us with a magical parable of coming out in "What Are You Waiting For?" This serves as a segue to the book's second half, Affirming the Community. Olivia Garrison upends the glorification of colonization with "Two-Spirit People and the Impact of Colonialism in California," while Jada Thompson, Jay Wang, and Carol Jacob do away with the false presumption of novelty of gender defiance with "Female Husbands," a lesson on transgender history in 18th and 19th century England and America.

We are reminded that resisting oppression in education is bounded neither by subject nor by age range with the final two lessons. "Yassifying Math With 'The Hips on the Drag Queen'" by El Chen with Cathery Yeh and B. E. Waid teaches counting using a picture book drag queen parade through San Francisco, while B. E. Waid and Tyrone Martinez-Black show how students can use trigonometry to explore equitable resource allocation with "2SLGBTQIA+ Community Centers: A Beacon of Hope."

This volume includes lessons for students of all ages, from preschool to high school and beyond. Its contributors range from academics to seasoned educators to a current middle school student. Each lesson offers new applications of and insights on the Gender Identity Complexities, Bridge to Thriving, and Historically Responsive Literacy Frameworks, which can be used to inform responsive, reparative pedagogy in many other cases besides. The lessons in this book may be deployed as they are, adapted for use as is necessary, or used as examples to inspire the creation of entirely distinct modules that are likewise responsive, celebratory, and affirming, three themes explored by educators and students who shared their experiences and analyses with us from across the country.

Many contend that crafting responsive education requires a deep-rooted respect for student autonomy and agency. To be responsive, educators must continually ask themselves, in M. Luebbert's words, "What are these young people telling you they need?" Our respondents emphasized that only what is recognized and honored may be celebrated. True celebration requires allowing trans* and gender-creative people to "share their stories," as B. Matthews points out, "rather than always having stories told about us," for people to be seen in what A. Daniels calls "all of our multitudes and all of our joyful, messy mix." Finally, affirming entails an attitude of care towards one another: "being there for someone," per E. Chen.

Each chapter is a testimonial to the importance of responsive, celebratory, and affirming pedagogies that are simultaneously tools for practitioners to take up, to modify, and to use. But this book is not merely a set of testimonials and tools. It is also a test. We are not testing the far-right ideologues who legislate against our existence because they have already failed, and history will condemn them accordingly. No, this volume is a test for you. It is a test for every educator, student, parent, neighbor, community member who comes across it. The contributors to this book have shared the importance of trans* and gender affirming education to their lives and communities and offered tools to help you practice it on your own. Whether to answer the call is now up to you. Whether a preschool class or a college symposium, whether a math lesson or a re-examination of American history, each and every educational space can either affirm the thriving of trans* and gender-creative youth or aid and abet in their oppression.

CONCLUSION

We acknowledge that, at this moment, these are not trivial choices for a teacher, parent, or community member to make. The transphobic far-right is organizing to make supporting trans* and gender-creative youth professionally, reputationally, and personally risky. But no matter who we are or what identities we hold, the harms created by this hatred will accrue most painfully not to us, those reading and writing this book, but the T*GY young people who might never have the chance to see anything like it. Those who may never see depictions of others like themselves except in the crudest and cruelest stereotypes. Those for whom the implementation of just a single affirming space might mean the difference between life and death.

The challenge that this book presents to you, reader, is to do what is necessary. To act decisively, regardless of the cost. To create the schools, communities, and world that we need. To struggle endlessly, courageously, and yes, joyously, to construct and defend the spaces that those students deserve. In a just world, creating spaces for students to thrive would involve neither courage nor risk. It is upon us to act defiantly today so such a world might exist tomorrow.

AFTERWORD

Mario I. Suárez

First and foremost, I would like to express deep gratitude to Dr. Kia Darling-Hammond and Dr. Bre Evans-Santiago for extending an invitation for me to write this afterword, as well as to each and every contributor to this book. It is an honor to write some of the last words you, the reader, will see before closing this book and going on about your life. Perhaps you came across this book because you are part of the queer and/or trans* community. Perhaps you came across this book because you have a loved one who is part of the community . . . or maybe you are an ally or striving to be a better one. Or, perhaps you came across this book as part of a professional development or book club at your school or school district. Whatever the reason—thank you for engaging with this critical work.

As a Mexican American trans man born and raised on the Texas-México border and as a former high school math teacher, I only wish this book existed when I was growing up and when I was a teacher. I now teach pre-service teachers, and as I teach about diversity and ways of being a more inclusive teacher, I always tell my students each semester that they have several choices after they leave my classroom: 1) They can leave my classroom and go about their life, and teach as if they did not learn anything about the educational disparities that minoritized youth face; 2) They can try to implement some of the things they learned in the class; and/or 3) They can always reach out to experts and find resources to continue growing as allies. I always hope they do the last two. However, I do not blame them if they are forced to do only the first—go about their life and rely only on the materials their schools and/or school districts adopt.

We are living in a state of tension in the field of education. We have so many teachers who are overworked and underpaid, and with one of the highest turnover rates we have seen ever in our teacher workforce.[1] At the same time, state legislatures are trying to pass anti-LGBTQ laws that render queer and trans* lives invisible and in danger.[2] As I said, I do not blame them if teachers are just trying to stay afloat in their profession. I really wish that choice did not come at such a high cost, though. In most cases, these choices lead to our queer and trans* youth with lower sense of belonging, or worse, suicidal attempts. The state where I teach and live—Utah—has one of the highest rates of suicide for queer and trans* youth, with almost half of

LGBTQ having suicidal ideation.³ My friend and colleague Dr. Boni Wozolek, and associates (2017), refer to this as the "school-to-coffin pipeline."

The majority of the research I read and work on can be very depressing, especially when studying the lives of trans* individuals like myself—trans* and gender-creative youth of color. It is tough to believe that, in 2023, not many books have done what this book does. The lessons in this book do the very opposite of most of what I read and write—they create spaces in our classrooms for our trans* and gender-creative youth to thrive, more than simply just existing and surviving. As a consumer of popular culture, I recently learned about the love story of Latinx social media stars Trino and Adam after photos from a shoot went viral.⁴ Trino and Adam's love story caught the eye of Matt Cullen, the creator of YouTube documentary series, "Our Queer Life." In a sit-down interview with the couple, Trino spoke about his tumultuous, estranged relationship with his family, who repeatedly bullied and harassed him as a child for being queer.⁵ Trino spoke to not needing validation from his family anymore, "You should've protected that young boy, not this grown man, 'cuz I can handle it. He couldn't handle it, you know what I'm saying. He couldn't handle it . . . I feel like right now what's going on with people embracing us. People don't even understand how it's been so healing for me, you know, 'cuz that's not my real life." Though gender identity and sexual orientation are different (though sometimes related), the words that Trino spoke really resonated with me.

Our children need us at a young age to affirm them, because when they get older, it may be too late. This is why this book is so important. It sparks the imagination of educators as a beginning to guide and foster trans* and gender-creative youth thriving. As I have told my students hundreds of times, I hope that you take some or all of what you have learned and implement it, and that you seek out resources that can continue to support you as an ally. If you are a trans* person, know that there are a lot of people working to make sure your world is much kinder and nicer than the one many of us grew up with.

Notes

1. Barnum, 2023; Choi, 2023
2. Izaguirre & Farrington, 2023; Kuchar, 2023
3. Takada, 2022
4. Crombet, 2023
5. Cullen, 2023

References

Barnum, M. (2023, March 6). Teacher turnover hits new highs across the U.S. *Chalkbeat*. https://www.chalkbeat.org/2023/3/6/23624340/teacher-turnover-leaving-the-profession-quitting-higher-rate

Choi, A. (2023, May 31). Teachers are calling it quits amid rising school violence, burnout and stagnating salaries. *CNN*. https://www.cnn.com/2023/05/31/us/teachers-quitting-shortage-stress-burnout-dg/index.html

Crombet, B. I. (2023, August 3). Chicano couple shines in photoshoot by Mexican photographer who wants to redefine queer love for Latinos. *Mitú*. https://wearemitu.com/latidomusic/henry-jimenez-mexican-photographer-gay-couple/

Cullen, M. (2023, June 25). *18-year gay relationship: 'My family still doesn't accept us'* [Video]. You Tube. https://www.youtube.com/watch?v=GqKUJHQhaII

Izaguirre, A., & Farrington, B. (2023, April 19). Florida expands 'Don't Say Gay'; House Oks anti-LGBTQ bills. *Associated Press*. https://apnews.com/article/desantis-florida-dont-say-gay-ban-684ed25a303f83208a89c556543183cb

Kuchar, S. (2023, January 27). A wave of anti-LGBTQ laws for schools in red states has Biden administration weighing a response. *USA Today*. https://www.usatoday.com/story/news/politics/2023/01/27/anti-lgbtq-laws-red-states-schools/10996463002/

Takada, L. (2022, April 6). 46% of lesbian, gay, or bisexual teens contemplated suicide in 2021, CDC says. *ABC 4 News*. https://www.abc4.com/news/local-news/46-of-lesbian-gay-or-bisexual-teens-contemplated-suicide-in-2021-cdc-says/#:~:text=According%20to%20a%20survey%20by,seriously%20considered%20suicide%20in%202021.

Wozolek, B., Wootton, L., & Demlow, A. (2017). The school-to-coffin pipeline: Queer youth, suicide, and living the in-between. *Cultural Studies <-> Critical Methodologies, 17*(5), 392–398. https://doi.org/10.1177/1532708616673659

APPENDIX A

Story Contributor Biographies

Each summary of biographical details below is from the storyteller and in their words.

Benjamin
My pronouns are he/they, and I'm a Black queer person. I am originally from Florida. Jacksonville, Florida to be exact. I reside now in the Washington, DC area. I am a marketing and communications strategist. Most of my work is done in digital media and communications for higher education institutions, fashion industry, nonprofits, or people who have compatible missions. I'm a mission-driven practitioner. My passions include education equality, queer liberation, and Black queer representation. I love fashion on the fun side. I love getting dressed up and going to events and seeing what's out there in the art world.

E. Chen
Hi! I'm El. I use they/them pronouns. I am a nonbinary lesbian tween. I am Chinese American. I have a 15-year-old sister, and a dog named Yuri. I love my friends. I love my teachers. My favorite subjects are STEM. I have not felt one gender since I was 3 years old. Kids at school tease me, and I am scared every day to go to the bathroom. Kids stare and push me out. Other kids at school have thrown pebbles at me. I try to explain my pronouns and they don't understand. This year has been the hardest. My family and I watch our local school board meetings. The angry words parents say at the school board meetings, I hear the same words in the playground. These angry words impact everyone. My hope is that we keep schools safe. Everyone should feel safe and being safe requires us to be seen, accepted, and loved for our full selves. I love drag queens because they are creative, imaginative, brilliant, and beautiful!!

A. Daniels
A. (they/she) has devoted her career in education to elevating the voices of her transgender sisters and siblings in order to center, celebrate and protect transgender youth. A white, queer, neurodivergent, nonbinary trans woman, A. loves being both a mirror and a window for adolescents as they figure out their identities and find their voices in the world. A. has taught middle and high school science, activism, sex education, robotics, engineering, algebra, and queer media at New York City schools for over ten years including at Brooklyn Friends, Bank Street School for Children, Manhattan Country School, and the John Hopkins Center for Talented Youth. Presenting her work at Tufts University, Bank Street College, Hunter College, Brooklyn College, Chapin School, Allen-Stevenson School, the Free Minds Free Peoples Conference, Math for America, the National Coalition of Girls Schools, and the Academy for Teachers, among other institutions, A. has a long history of helping others teach about social justice. A. was one of the co-founders of the NYC Trans Educator Network and has served on several boards. Their work has also contributed to Black Lives Matter at NYC Schools. She passionately believes that science and math can be incredibly powerful tools to educate for liberation.

B. Flores
My pronouns are they/them/ellx. I am of Latinx descent. My family's from Mexico, I am a first-generation college student and I teach 7th and 8th graders at a K-8 school. I identify as queer, transgender, and nonbinary.

D. Hughes
I'm a Black trans male and a student at San Francisco State University. I began my transition about 10 years ago physically and came out about maybe when I was a freshman in high school, I think maybe 7 years ago. I'm also heavyset, but I more so look at that as muscle because of my physical laboring job and identify myself as someone who pushes themself until they no longer can, mentally struggling, diagnosed with severe depression and anxiety.

K. James
For this project, my chosen name is K. James and my pronouns are she/her/they/them. I am Caucasian of mainly Irish, Welsh, and German ancestry and descend from a working-class immigrant background. I currently identify as gender-fluid and trans, in the literal sense where it means, "change." I live change.

S. Javitz
My relevant identity here is nonbinary. I've got other queer identities as well.

STORY CONTRIBUTOR BIOGRAPHIES

B. Kennedy

I am a transgender author, educator, and activist who grew up in rural Maryland and later received both my BS and M.Ed. from The University of Vermont. I am currently pursuing a PhD education studies at UC San Diego, where my work focuses on equity policy, investigating and supporting gender identity development in early childhood, and helping educators to create queer and trans* affirming curriculum and classrooms. I am a sought-after public speaker, guest lecturer, and consultant on issues of gender diversity and education. I am a national facilitator with Welcoming Schools, a Board Member for Trans Youth Liberation, and a youth mentor at San Diego Pride. I have collaborated with The National Center for Transgender Equality, Planned Parenthood, Gender Odyssey, Bernie Sanders' office, and other organizations, and have been published in diverse outlets including multiple books, several academic journals, HuffPost, NPR, and more. My partner Becca and I have three cats, a three-legged pitbull, and a rotating crew of foster animals. Together we are passionate about good food, good music, and being good to others.

M. Luebbert

My pronouns are they/them/theirs and I have been a teacher in the School District of Philadelphia for 7 years. I am white, queer, and trans/nonbinary, as well as a lifelong Philadelphian. I started my career as a cisgender queer woman stuck in the closet, but eventually came out and changed my title to Mx. I live and work in the Kensington neighborhood, and I teach at a comprehensive neighborhood high school.

B. Matthews

I use they/them pronouns. And I identify as a trans masculine, genderqueer, non-binary person. Any of those words work, I really just identify as a person who has a body and who might be different from other people. I'm also white. I am currently the manager of diversity, equity, inclusion, and access at the National Youth Development Organization. I work for the National Office. We support our affiliates, which are in 24 states and Washington DC currently. I work specifically in increasing access to summer overnight programs like sleepaway kind of camps, for folks who have been historically excluded. Our priority populations are youth of different ethnic backgrounds because camping has historically been a white thing. Youth from lower socioeconomic backgrounds, youth with disabilities, and youth who are LGBTQ2S+ identified.

M. Rice

I am 53, and a trans guy. I was assigned female at birth, and I began my social transition when I was 21 in 1992, and I began my medical transition in 1993, when I was 24. I am white, and I have a college degree, as far as other social locations, things that are important. I am a person with a hidden disability. And I am a parent of a profoundly developmentally different kid. My son is not conversational. My superpower is translating the world to him and him to the world. I'm a doctoral student and I'm doing my dissertation on the experiences of trans* and nonbinary teachers in K-12 education. I just finished my 16th year teaching, and most of those years were in Charlotte, North Carolina, but I'm currently in New Jersey.

V. Zepeda

My pronouns are she/her/hers/ella, my identity is pansexual. My gender expression is androgynous. It's where I identify as having female and male characteristics on the outside with my style. I identify as Latinx and part of the Latino community.

APPENDIX B

Teaching Routines, Scaffolds, and Tools

Analyzing Primary Sources:
- **Blank Guide** – https://drive.google.com/file/d/1byZAkWkxE6ZmYl4zYAXRgDzXk8X Z_e5U/view?usp=drive_link
- **Teacher's Guide** – https://drive.google.com/file/d/1bpbpE8e8_0VrN3QOUigJIPaa5MBK913D/view?usp=drive_link

Body Scan Exercises:
- **Ray Lewey** – https://insighttimer.com/raylewey/guided-meditations/trans-embodiment-coming-home-to-ourselves
- **Mindful Schools** – https://drive.google.com/file/d/1iKY05ReW0ru5qvxVG1VmWNxrljRs0Bv/view?usp=drive_link
- **Vanessa Marrufo** – https://www.youtube.com/watch?v=e0f9wa2SUX0
- **Alli Simon** – https://www.youtube.com/watch?v=5qHC1-KCgIM

Box Breathing:
- **Conscious Works** – https://www.youtube.com/watch?v=n6RbW2LtdFs
- **Headspace** – https://www.youtube.com/watch?v=a7uQXDkxEtM

Chunk and Chew
- https://leadinglearningmatters.com/chunk-chew-giving-learners-processing-time/

Cooperative Learning Strategies
- https://sites.google.com/a/emints.org/cooperative-learning-strategies/page2

Creating a "Container" for Courage and Safety

- https://www.mindfulschools.org/inspiration/creating-a-safe-container-student-community-agreements/
- https://www.edutopia.org/blog/build-an-anti-racist-classroom-joshua-block

Exit Ticket

- https://www.structural-learning.com/post/exit-tickets#:~:text=What%20are%20Exit%20Tickets%3F,they%20are%20teaching%20in%20class

Five Senses Brainstorm

- http://readysetbrainstorm.weebly.com/the-five-senses.html

Gallery Walk

- https://www.edutopia.org/blog/enliven-class-discussion-with-gallery-walks-rebecca-alber
- https://youtu.be/XH63YrzduOM

Group Work

- https://uwaterloo.ca/centre-for-teaching-excellence/catalogs/tip-sheets/implementing-group-work-classroom

"I Am" Poem

- https://www.readwritethink.org/sites/default/files/resources/lesson_images/lesson391/I-am-poem.pdf

Identity Wheels

- **Personal Identity Wheel** – https://sites.lsa.umich.edu/inclusive-teaching/personal-identity-wheel/
- **Social Identity Wheel** – https://sites.lsa.umich.edu/ inclusive-teaching/social-identity-wheel/

Jamboard

- http://jamboard.google.com/

Jigsaw Method

- https://youtu.be/euhtXUgBEts
- See also Aronson, E., Stephan, C., Sikes, J., Blaney, N., & Snapp, M. (1978). *The jigsaw classroom*. Sage.

Journaling
- https://journey.cloud/reflective-journal

Literature Circle
- https://www.lauracandler.com/wp-content/uploads/2018/06/circle.pdf

Monitoring Chart
- https://resources.corwin.com/5practices-highschool/student-resources/charts-and-templates

Notice and Wonder
- https://mathforall.edc.org/routines-for-mathematical-thinking-engagement/

Padlet
- https://padlet.help/l/en/article/f5of9fy9lc-how-do-i-create-a-padlet

Quick Write (and other short writing practices)
- https://www.edutopia.org/article/power-short-writing-assignments

See, Think, Wonder
- https://pz.harvard.edu/resources/see-think-wonder

Shoulder Partners
- https://sites.google.com/a/emints.org/cooperative-learning-strategies/shoulder-partner-discussion

Smith and Stein's Five Practices:
- Resource 1 – https://www.sfusdmath.org/5-practices-for-orchestrating-productive-math-discussions.html
- Resource 2 – https://www.utdanacenter.org/sites/default/files/2019-07/Greenlee_CAMT_Teaching_Elementary_Students.pdf

Strategies and Struggles
- https://docs.google.com/document/d/1FJDoUHPzkBLZpncXudgRVGddJhFNmd7t/edit?usp=drive_link&ouid=100454804064360656722&rtpof=true&sd=true

Think Pair Share

- https://www.youtube.com/watch?v=Mig4olzUy4M

Wheel of Power/Privilege

- https://www.instagram.com/p/CEFiUShhpUT/?utm_source=ig_web_button_share_sheet
- https://www.flickr.com/photos/sylviaduckworth/50500299716/

Wow, Worry, Wonder Rubric

- https://docs.google.com/document/d/1k-JvM9Oiv5SaF45Whqd4MZAf7E9ER3Tr/edit?usp=drive_link&ouid=100454804064360656722&rtpof=true&sd=true

APPENDIX C

Editor Recommendations for Further Learning and Exploration

THIS IS A STARTER list of resources to help readers ground themselves in trans* and gender-creative community experiences and needs. We are grateful to Melinda Mangin (2020) and have pulled some resources from her beautifully curated guide. Descriptions are largely taken directly from each resource's website.

Organizations with Educational Resources & Tools

Welcoming Schools, a project of the Human Rights Campaign Foundation
https://welcomingschools.org/

Welcoming Schools is a comprehensive national bias-based bullying prevention program that provides LGBTQ+ and gender inclusive professional development training, lesson plans, booklists, and resources specifically designed for educators and youth-serving professionals. The program uses an intersectional, anti-racist lens dedicated to designing actionable policies and practices.

Learning For Justice, A project of the Southern Poverty Law Center
https://www.splcenter.org/learning-for-justice

Learning for Justice seeks to uphold the Southern Poverty Law Center's mission: to be a catalyst for racial justice in the South and beyond, working in partnership with communities to dismantle white supremacy, strengthen intersectional movements, and advance the human rights of all people. This mission is supported through focused work with educators, students, caregivers, and communities.

Gender Spectrum

https://www.genderspectrum.org/

Gender Spectrum's mission is to create a gender-inclusive world for all children and youth. To accomplish this, we help families, organizations, and institutions increase their understanding of gender and consider the implications that evolving views have for each of us.

GLSEN

https://www.glsen.org/

GLSEN works to ensure that LGBTQ students are able to learn and grow in a school environment free from bullying and harassment. Together we can transform our nation's schools into the safe and affirming environment all youth deserve.

National SOGIE Center

https://sogiecenter.org/

The National Center for Youth with Diverse Sexual Orientation, Gender Identity & Expression (The National SOGIE Center) provides a centralized site for accessing resources on providing culturally responsive care to children, youth, young adults with diverse sexual orientation, gender identity, and gender expression (SOGIE) and their families across systems, including child welfare, juvenile justice, mental health (including school mental health), substance use systems, and housing and homelessness.

Teaching LGBTQ History

https://www.lgbtqhistory.org/

This site serves as a comprehensive reference hub for information regarding the FAIR Education Act, as well as for History Framework Lesson Plans and General LGBTQ Lesson Plans, and resources to support teachers as they work with the new content required by the FAIR Education Act. We are honored to work together with you to help California's history and social sciences education be more Fair, Accurate, Inclusive and Respectful for all K-12 students.

RECOMMENDATIONS FOR FURTHER LEARNING

Organizations That Provide Services & Advocacy

National Center for Transgender Equality

https://transequality.org/

NCTE works to change policy to advance transgender equality, providing a powerful advocacy presence in Washington, DC.

PFLAG

https://pflag.org/

PFLAG supports LGBTQ+ families, friends, and allies through a network of local chapters, support groups, and educational activities.

Trans Youth Equality Foundation

www.transyouthequality.org/

The Trans Youth Equality Foundation provides education, advocacy and support for transgender, nonbinary, and gender non-conforming children and youth and their families. Their mission is to share information about the unique needs of this community, partnering with families, educators, and service providers to help foster a healthy, caring, and safe environment for all children they serve.

Transgender Training Institute

www.transgendertraininginstitute.com

TTI leads professional development and personal growth trainings that provide participants with information and skills needed to be better prepared to affirm the transgender and non-binary people in their lives.

The Trevor Project

www.thetrevorproject.org/

The Trevor Project provides 24/7 crisis intervention and suicide prevention services to LGBTQ+ young people under age 25.

Other Resources

Digital Transgender Archive

https://www.digitaltransgenderarchive.net/

An online hub for digitized historical materials, born-digital materials, and information on archival holdings throughout the world.

Gender and Family Project - Ackerman Institute for the Family

www.genderandfamilyproject.org

The Gender & Family Project (GFP) empowers youth, families, and communities by providing gender affirmative services, training, and research. GFP promotes gender inclusivity as a form of social justice in all the systems involved in the life of the family.

Them Magazine

https://www.them.us/

Them is the award-winning authority on what it means to be LGBTQ+ today — and tomorrow. From in-depth storytelling on the fight for LGBTQ+ rights to intimate profiles of queer cultural vanguards, we're a platform for all of the bold and rebellious ways that LGBTQ+ people are reshaping our world every day.

Trans Language Primer

https://translanguageprimer.com/

This primer is an attempt to document the movement to express and identify the complexity of gender while acknowledging its history and intersections.

Trans Reads

https://transreads.org/

The world's largest collection of free trans-focused literature.

US Department of Education, Office for Civil Rights (OCR)

https://www2.ed.gov/about/offices/list/ocr/aboutocr.html

The mission of the Office for Civil Rights is to ensure equal access to education and to promote educational excellence throughout the nation through vigorous enforcement of civil rights. Civil rights complaints can be filed online and anonymously by any person or organization if they believe someone has experienced a violation of their civil rights.

Books For Educators

about Gender Identity Justice in Schools and Communities - sj Miller - 2019 - Teachers College Press

What is gender identity justice, why does it matter, and what are the implications for not doing this work in today's schools? This premiere book in the new Teachers College Press series *School : Questions* carefully walks readers through both theory and practice to equip them with the skills needed to bring gender identity justice into classrooms, schools, and ultimately society. The text looks into the root causes and ways to change the conditions that have created gender identity injustice. It opens up spaces where evolving, indeterminate gender identities will be understood and recognized as asset-based, rich sources for learning literacy and literacy learning. As educators take up the strategies mapped out across this text, they will learn how to foster school environments that aid all students in becoming agents for social change. This text is the first of its kind to address gender identity in teacher education with pathways to take up the work in communities and beyond.

Everything You Ever Wanted to Know about Trans (But Were Afraid to Ask) - Brynn Tannehill - 2018 - Jessica Kingsley Publishers

This book aims to break down deeply held misconceptions about trans people across all aspects of life, from politics, law, and culture, to science, religion, and mental health, to provide readers with a deeper understanding of what it means to be trans.

Gender: A Graphic Guide - Meg-John Barker - 2020 - Icon Books

We'll look at how gender has been 'done' differently, from patriarchal societies to trans communities—and how it has been viewed differently—from biological arguments for sex difference to cultural arguments about received gender norms. We'll dive into complex and shifting ideas about masculinity and femininity, look at non-binary, trans, and fluid genders, and examine the intersection of experiences of gender with people's race, sexuality, class, disability and more.

Tackling current debates and tensions, which can divide communities and even cost lives, we'll look to the past and the future to ask how might we approach gender differently, in more socially constructive, caring ways.

Gender: Your Guide: A Gender-Friendly Primer on What to Know, What to Say, and What to Do in the New Gender Culture - Lee Airton - 2019 - Adams Media

From the differences among gender identity, gender expression, and sex, to the use of gender-neutral pronouns like singular they/them, to thinking about your own participation in gender, *Gender: Your Guide* serves as "a warm, inviting guide to a complicated area" (*The Globe and Mail*, Toronto). Professor and gender diversity advocate Lee Airton, PhD, explains how gender works in everyday life; how to use accurate terminology to refer to transgender, non-binary, and/or gender non-conforming individuals; and how to ask when you aren't sure what to do or say. It provides the information you need to talk confidently and compassionately about gender diversity, whether simply having a conversation or going to bat as an advocate.

How to They/Them: A Visual Guide to Nonbinary Pronouns and the World of Gender Fluidity - Stuart Getty - 2020 - Sasquatch Books

What does nonbinary really mean? What is gender nonconforming? And isn't *they* a plural pronoun? In this charming and disarming guide, a real-life *they*-using genderqueer writer unpacks all your burning questions in a fun, visual way. No soapboxes or divisive comment-section wars here!

Sometimes funny, sometimes serious, always human, this gender-friendly primer will get you up to speed. It's about more than just bathrooms and pronouns—this is about gender expression and the freedom to choose how to identify. While *they* might only be for some, that freedom is for everyone!

Transgender Students in Elementary School: Creating an Affirming and Inclusive School Culture - Melinda Mangin - 2020 - Harvard Education Press

Transgender Students in Elementary School offers guidance to educators who want to provide a supportive school culture and climate for transgender and gender-expansive students. The book provides recommendations for creating learning environments that facilitate all students' sense of belonging and reduce the constraints inherent in binary gender norms.

Through this book, teachers and school leaders can deepen their understanding about *why* they need to make schools gender-inclusive and *how* to make it happen. Focusing on case studies of five schools, Melinda M. Mangin provides real-life quotes and vignettes that candidly illustrate the learning curve of leaders, staff, and families. These stories demonstrate both the successes and challenges of creating affirming school environments for transgender and gender-expansive students.

You Can't Be Neutral on a Moving Train: A Personal History - Howard Zinn - 2018 - Beacon Press

Howard Zinn—activist, historian, and author of *A People's History of the United States*—was a participant in and chronicler of some of the landmark struggles for racial and economic justice in US history. In his memoir, *You Can't Be Neutral on a Moving Train*, Zinn reflects on more than 30 years of fighting for social change, from his teenage years as a laborer in Brooklyn to teaching at Spelman College, where he emerged in the civil rights movement as a powerful voice for justice. A former bombardier in World War II, he later became an outspoken antiwar activist, spirited protestor, and champion of civil disobedience. Throughout his life, Zinn was unwavering in his belief that "small acts, when multiplied by millions of people, can transform the world." With a foreword from activist and scholar Keeanga-Yamahtta Taylor, this revised edition will inspire a new generation of readers to believe that change is possible.

Children's Books

Alex and Alex - Ziggy Hanaor - 2022 - Cicada Books

Alex and Alex have lots of things in common. They love playing and dressing up and building things. They also are very different from one another. Alex is very messy, and Alex is very tidy; Alex likes running and kicking a ball and Alex likes reading and dreaming. After a trip to the museum goes a little bit awry, Alex and Alex have some cooling off time. But they always make up because Alex really really really really really really REALLY. . . . likes Alex!

This is a book for very young readers introducing ideas of tolerance and friendship in a completely non-gendered way. Neither character is identified as a boy or a girl, and the activities that each one enjoys is a mix of traditional 'boy' and 'girl' things. Aimed at children who are just at the cusp of gender awareness and role-play, it provides a much-needed counterbalance to more traditional, binary pre-school literature.

Calvin – JR and Vanessa Ford - 2021 - G.P. Putnam's Sons Books for Young Readers

Calvin has always been a boy, even if the world sees him as a girl. He knows who he is in his heart and in his mind, but he hasn't yet told his family. Finally, he can wait no longer: "I'm not a girl," he tells his family. "I'm a boy—a boy in my heart and in my brain." Quick to support him, his loving family takes Calvin shopping for the swim trunks he's always wanted and back-to-school clothes and a new haircut that helps him look and feel like the boy he's always known himself to be. As the first day of school approaches, he's nervous and the "what-ifs" gather up inside him. But as his friends and teachers rally around him and he tells them his name, all his "what-ifs" begin to melt away.

Inspired by the authors' own transgender child and accompanied by warm and triumphant illustrations, this authentic and personal text promotes kindness and empathy, offering a poignant and inclusive back-to-school message: all should feel safe, respected, and welcomed.

Felix Ever After - Kacen Callender - 2020 - Balzer + Bray

Felix Love has never been *in* love—and, yes, he's painfully aware of the irony. He desperately wants to know what it's like and why it seems so easy for everyone but him to find someone. What's worse is that, even though he is proud of his identity, Felix also secretly fears that he's one marginalization too many—Black, queer, and transgender—to ever get his own happily-ever-after.

When an anonymous student begins sending him transphobic messages—after publicly posting Felix's deadname alongside images of him before he transitioned—Felix comes up with a plan for revenge. What he didn't count on: his catfish scenario landing him in a quasi–love triangle. . . .

But as he navigates his complicated feelings, Felix begins a journey of questioning and self-discovery that helps redefine his most important relationship: how he feels about himself.

Felix Ever After is an honest and layered story about identity, falling in love, and recognizing the love you deserve.

Gracefully Grayson - Ami Polonsky - 2014 - Little, Brown Books for Young Readers

Grayson Sender has been holding onto a secret for what seems like forever: "he" is a girl on the inside, stuck in the wrong gender's body. The weight of this secret is crushing, but sharing it would mean facing ridicule, scorn, rejection, or worse. Despite the risks, Grayson's true self itches to break free. Will new strength from an unexpected friendship and a caring teacher's wisdom be enough to help Grayson step into the spotlight she was born to inhabit?

I Am Jazz - Jessica Herthel and Jazz Jennings - 2014 - Dial Books

From the time she was 2 years old, Jazz knew that she had a girl's brain in a boy's body. She loved pink and dressing up as a mermaid and didn't feel like herself in boys' clothing. This confused her family, until they took her to a doctor who said that Jazz was transgender and that she was born that way. Jazz's story is based on her real-life experience and she tells it in a simple, clear way that will be appreciated by picture book readers, their parents, and teachers.

If You're a Kid Like Gavin: The True Story of a Young Trans Activist Hardcover - Gavin Grimm - 2022 - Katherine Tegen Books

A celebratory and empowering story from young trans activist Gavin Grimm, two-time Stonewall Award–winning and Newbery Honor–winning author Kyle Lukoff, and illustrator J Yang follows the true story of how a young boy stood up for himself—and made history along the way. A *Publishers Weekly* and *Kirkus* Best Book of the Year.

RECOMMENDATIONS FOR FURTHER LEARNING

Jacob's New Dress - Sarah and Ian Hoffman - 2020 - Albert Whitman & Company

An affirming story about gender nonconformity.

Jacob loves playing dress-up when he can be anything he wants to be. Some kids at school say he can't wear "girl" clothes, but Jacob wants to wear a dress to school. Can he convince his parents to let him wear what he wants? This heartwarming story speaks to the unique challenges faced by children who don't identify with traditional gender roles.

Katerina Cruickshanks - Daniel Gray-Barnett - 2022 - Scribble US

Katerina Cruickshanks is a wild child, a trickster, and a ringleader. But when they wreak some serious chaos, their friends decide their shenanigans have gone too far and say, "No more!"

Brimming with humor and warmth, Katerina shows us that there's no such thing as being too much; it's just a matter of finding the friends who will love you as you are.

One of A Kind, Like Me/Único Como Yo - Laurin Mayeno - 2016 - Blood Orange Press

Tomorrow is the school parade, and Danny knows exactly what he will be: a princess. Mommy supports him 100%, and they race to the thrift store to find his costume. It's almost closing time—will Danny find the costume of his dreams in time? *One of A Kind, Like Me/Único Como Yo* is a sweet story about unconditional love and the beauty of individuality. It's a unique book that lifts up children who don't fit gender stereotypes and reflects the power of a loving and supportive community.

Lily and Dunkin - Donna Gephart - 2016 - Delacorte Press

Lily Jo McGrother, born Timothy McGrother, is a girl. But being a girl is not so easy when you look like a boy, especially when you're in the eighth grade.

Dunkin Dorfman, birth name Norbert Dorfman, is dealing with bipolar disorder and has just moved from the New Jersey town he's called home for the past 13 years. This would be hard enough, but the fact that he is also hiding from a painful secret makes it even worse.

One summer morning, Lily Jo McGrother meets Dunkin Dorfman, and their lives forever change.

My Sister, Daisy - Adria Karlsson - 2021 - Capstone Press

Daisy's older brother is thrilled when he gets a new sibling. They are best buddies who do everything together. But in kindergarten, things change. His sibling tells him she is a girl and wants to be called Daisy. Daisy's brother must adjust to the change—including what it means for him and their relationship. A powerful, moving picture book based on a true story, *My Sister, Daisy* handles a sensitive subject with warmth and love.

Sam Is My Sister - Ashley Rhodes-Courter - 2021 - Albert Whitman & Company

Evan loves being big brother to Sam and Finn. They do everything together—go fishing, climb trees, and play astronauts. But lately, Evan notices that he and Sam don't look like brothers anymore. Sam wants to have long hair, and even asks to wear a dress on the first day of school. As time goes by, Evan comes to understand why Sam wants to look like a girl—because Sam is a girl. Sam is transgender. And just like always, Sam loves to dream with Evan and Finn about going to the moon together. Based on one family's real-life experiences, this heartwarming story of a girl named Sam and the brothers who love and support her will resonate with readers everywhere.

Sparkle Boy - Lesléa Newman - 2017 - Lee and Low books

Casey loves to play with his blocks, puzzles, and dump truck, but he also loves things that sparkle, shimmer, and glitter. When his older sister, Jessie, shows off her new shimmery skirt, Casey wants to wear a shimmery skirt too. When Jessie comes home from a party with glittery nails, Casey wants glittery nails too. And when Abuelita visits wearing an armful of sparkly bracelets, Casey gets one to wear, just like Jessie. The adults in Casey's life embrace his interests, but Jessie isn't so sure. Boys aren't supposed to wear sparkly, shimmery, glittery things. Then, when older boys at the library tease Casey for wearing "girl" things, Jessie realizes that Casey has the right to be himself and wear whatever he wants. Why can't both she and Casey love all things shimmery, glittery, and sparkly? Here is a sweet, heartwarming story about acceptance, respect, and the freedom to be yourself in a world where any gender expression should be celebrated. Sparkly things are for everyone to enjoy!

The Witch Boy - Molly Knox Ostertag - 2017 - Graphix

In 13-year-old Aster's family, all the girls are raised to be witches, while boys grow up to be shapeshifters. Anyone who dares cross those lines is exiled. Unfortunately for Aster, he still hasn't shifted . . . and he's still fascinated by witchery, no matter how forbidden it might be. When a mysterious danger threatens the other boys, Aster knows he can help—as a witch. It will take the encouragement of a new friend, the non-magical and non-conforming Charlie, to convince Aster to try practicing his skills. And it will require even more courage to save his family . . . and be truly himself.

RECOMMENDATIONS FOR FURTHER LEARNING

Timid - Harry Woodgate - 2022 - little bee books

Timmy loves to perform, but only when there isn't an audience! When Timmy feels most nervous, their shy inner lion roars all their confidence away. This gorgeous, uplifting picture book by British Book Award winner and Stonewall Book Award Honoree Harry Woodgate shines a spotlight on childhood anxiety. With bravery, courage, and friendship, Timmy learns to embrace his inner lion and follow their dreams.

When Aidan Became a Brother - Kyle Lukoff - 2019 - Lee & Low Books.

This sweet and groundbreaking picture book, winner of the 2020 Stonewall Book Award, celebrates the changes in a transgender boy's life, from his initial coming-out to becoming a big brother.

Understanding Bodies, Gender, & Gender Identity

Being You: A First Conversation About Gender - Megan Madison and Jessica Ralli - 2021 - Rise x Penguin Workshop

Developed by experts in the fields of early childhood and activism against injustice, this topic-driven board book offers clear, concrete language and beautiful imagery that young children can grasp and adults can leverage for further discussion.

While young children are avid observers and questioners of their world, adults often shut down or postpone conversations on complicated topics because it's hard to know where to begin. Research shows that talking about issues like race and gender from the age of 2 not only helps children understand what they see, but also increases self-awareness, self-esteem, and allows them to recognize and confront things that are unfair, like discrimination and prejudice.

This second book in the series begins the conversation on gender, with a supportive approach that considers both the child and the adult. Stunning art accompanies the simple and interactive text, and the backmatter offers additional resources and ideas for extending this discussion.

Every Body is a Rainbow: A Kid's Guide to Bodies Across the Gender Spectrum - Caroline Carter - 2023 - Rainbow Kids Press

Every child has an amazing body that is all their own! Each one is a unique shape, size, and color and has a unique mix of parts, identities, and expressions. *Every Body is a Rainbow: A Kid's Guide to Bodies Across the Gender Spectrum* celebrates the vast rainbow of bodies and identities—from nonbinary, to intersex, to multiple genders and expressions—and shows readers that every body is beautifully diverse and has value. This book is for kids and families of ALL genders, abilities, and expressions who want to understand themselves and learn more about the amazing bodies across the gender spectrum! Transgender children, or families with a transgender child, will find this book especially affirming!

The Gender Wheel - School Edition: A Story About Bodies and Gender for Every Body - Maya Christina Gonzalez - 2018 - Reflection Press

A picture book journey through the Gender Wheel. This School Edition takes the original book, *The Gender Wheel* (2017), and puts clothes on all the kids to be more conducive to school environments. It is a powerful opportunity for kids to understand the origins of the current binary gender system, how we can learn from nature to see the truth that has always existed, and revision a new story that includes room for all bodies and genders. The Gender Wheel offers a nature-based, holistic non-Western framework of gender in a kid-friendly way. Also included are Teacher Tips on how to hold a holistic perspective on gender in the classroom. www.genderwheel.com

It's Perfectly Normal: Changing Bodies, Growing Up, Sex, Gender, and Sexual Health - Robie H. Harris - 2021 - Candlewick

With more than 1.5 million copies in print, *It's Perfectly Normal* has been a trusted resource on sexuality for more than 25 years. Rigorously vetted by experts, this is the most ambitiously updated edition yet, featuring to-the-minute information and language accompanied by new and refreshed art.

Some Bodies - Sophie Kennen- 2022 - Sleeping Bear Press

Our bodies! Our amazing, astounding, and all-around awesome bodies! Bodies come in all shapes, sizes, and colors, and can do extraordinary things. Our bodies are uniquely our own yet they connect us to the world around us in so many ways. Through playful rhymes and colorful engaging artwork, all the things that make our bodies special—from the texture of our hair to the color of our eyes—are celebrated. This sweet and inclusive book encourages young readers to acknowledge and accept differences, and offers the perfect opportunity to open up conversations about body acceptance. Every body is different and all bodies are good. Back matter includes tips and conversation starters for parents and educators to use with children.

Who Are You?: The Kid's Guide to Gender Identity - Brook Pessin-Whedbee - 2016 - Jessica Kingsley Publishers.

This brightly illustrated children's book provides a straightforward introduction to gender for anyone aged 5–8. It presents clear and direct language for understanding and talking about how we experience gender: our bodies, our expression, and our identity. An interactive three-layered wheel included in the book is a simple, yet powerful, tool to clearly demonstrate the difference between our body, how we express ourselves through our clothes and hobbies, and our gender identity.

ABOUT THE AUTHORS

About the Editors

Dr. Kia Darling-Hammond (she/they) is author of the *Bridge to Thriving Framework*© and co-author of the award-winning book *The Civil Rights Road to Deeper Learning: Five Essentials for Equity*. As CEO of the education and research firm Wise Chipmunk LLC, Dr. Kia leverages over 25 years of experience in youth development, education, and organizational leadership to offer thriving-focused research, advising, coaching, and public speaking, as well as designs for professional learning, curriculum development, and organizational growth. Her work emphasizes the importance of combining the science of learning and development with healing- and transformative justice to promote an evolution toward thriving for all. This approach is grounded in the knowledge that innovation driven by the wisdom of those furthest from power is key to improving everyone's lives. Dr. Kia has published work in *Equity and Excellence in Education, Liberal Education, Nonprofit Quarterly*, and *The Lancet Regional Health - Americas*, and holds service commitments as a member of Congresswoman Bonnie Watson Coleman's Black Mental Health Brain Trust, as a contributing scholar and advisor to Sports Equity Lab, and as a member of the Wild Seed Liberation Land Board of Directors.

Dr. Bre Evans-Santiago (she/her) is an award-winning author, Chair, and Associate Professor in the Teacher Education Department at California State University, Bakersfield. Her research focuses on culturally sustaining pedagogy and practices in TK–8 schools. Dr. Evans-Santiago also has research experience in improvement science as it relates to Residencies and educational programs. Her current research projects include but are not limited to, Black Teacher Residencies and Black, Indigenous, and People of Color issues in education, which also include intersectionalities connected to Queer BIPOC in schools. Dr. Evans-Santiago is also the Co-Director of the California State University Center for Transformational Educator Preparation Programs where she leads and supports CSU campuses to recruit, prepare, and retain teachers of color across California. Her award-winning book *Mistakes We Have Made: Implications for Social Justice Educators* provides a vulnerable perspective of everyday scenarios and strategies for teachers of all ages to reflect upon while teaching with a social justice framework. Her accolades include the 2022-23 Faculty Leadership and Service Award, the 2023 CSUB Unity Award, and the 2022 Administrator of the Year Award for Professor of Education.

About the Authors

Danelle Adeniji is an advanced doctoral candidate in the PhD Curriculum and Instruction Studies program at the University of North Texas. Their research is situated at the intersection of queer, elementary, and urban education. To study the connection between Black queer teachers and queering Afrofuturism, their research centers around how traditional teacher preparation programs can draw from a Black queer Afrofuturist lens to co-construct curricula and pedagogical practices, where everyone has access to dream and see their future.

El Chen (they/them) is author of the short story "What Are You Waiting For?" and a chapter about counting entitled "Yassifying Math With 'The Hips on the Drag Queen.'" El's favorite subjects are in STEM fields. A nonbinary lesbian tween, they have not felt one gender since they were 3 years old. El is dedicated to helping to keep schools safe and believes that everyone should feel safe, which requires them to be seen, accepted, and loved for their full selves.

Ana Cornejo (she/her) is a first-generation immigrant from Mexico. Currently, she is a doctoral candidate in the Doctoral Program in Educational Leadership at CSU Bakersfield. She has served her community for 7 years as a public school educator. Ana is passionate about education and believes that every child should have access to an education that is rigorous, enriching, and empowering.

K. Elliott (he/they) is a white, queer, neuro-sparkly, trans human—an advocate, educator, organizer, and co-conspirator for movements led by young people radically transforming our world. Their work challenges organizations and community systems to reimagine authentic partnership with young people, and to shift power, policies, and practices towards racial and social justice. Elliott holds a Bachelor's in Special Education, a Master's in Social Work, and years of direct service and leadership experience across youth sectors. For him, thriving feels like being rooted in body, mind, and spirit—in having expansive space for dreaming—and being connected in love and community.

Bobbi Evans-Santiago is a Trans Man who earned his master's degree in educational counseling for Student Affairs from California State University Bakersfield in May 2023. Bobbi obtained his Bachelor of Science in Political Science, a minor in Criminal Justice, and a Minor in Middle Eastern and South Asian Studies from Illinois State University. Bobbi currently works at California State University, Bakersfield, in the Department of Athletics and is openly out on campus. His hobbies include painting and going to the beach.

ABOUT THE AUTHORS

Wendy Garay is a middle school teacher and LGBTQ+ Pride Club adviser. She also serves as her district's first LGBTQ+ Resource Support Provider. In addition, Wendy is involved with several community organizations and collaboratives that focus on providing safe and equitable learning environments for LGBTQ+ students and their allies. A lifelong learner, Wendy is pursuing her doctorate in Educational Leadership from California State University, Bakersfield.

Olivia Garrison (they/she) is currently teaching 10th grade World History in the Kern High School District. In 2023, they were selected as the Don Romesburg Prize winner and the 2023 California Council for the Social Studies (CCSS) Equity, Inclusion and Social Justice Educator Awardee. They are the Pride Club (GSA) advisor at their site and a member of the GSA Advisor's Committee. Olivia also serves on the Kern High School District Social Studies Leadership Team developing curriculum and guiding professional development for the district. One of their goals as an educator is to facilitate the creation and implementation of LGBTQ+ inclusive curriculum that celebrates gender and sexuality diversity throughout California and beyond. As a non-binary person, Olivia is particularly devoted to protecting trans* youth.

Bethany Gonzales is an elementary school teacher from California who prides herself on creating lessons that actively engage students both academically and socially-emotionally. In addition, she helps guide her district in using and incorporating up-to-date technology in the classroom and is an avid fan of project-based learning. Having a master's degree in Curriculum & Instruction with an undergraduate focus on liberal studies and American Sign Language, Bethany continues to work towards providing inclusion for all in classrooms across the country.

Carol Jacob (she/her) earned her Master of Public Health degree in Health Promotion & Behavioral Sciences at UTHealth School of Public Health at Houston with certificates in health disparities as well as maternal and child health. During her MPH, Carol worked on adolescent sexual health research projects in high teen birth rate areas in the greater Houston Area and was the internal chair for the student outREACH student organization. In addition, Carol is also an Albert Schweitzer Fellow-for-Life; her project focused on healthy relationships and sexual health education in adolescent teen girls at New Hope Housing. Carol now applies what she has learned with her education and experience in her current role as Program Director for the Albert Schweitzer Fellowship to assist current fellows in program development, management, and using an intersectional lens when working with communities.

Benjamin C. Kennedy (he/him) is a transgender author, educator, and activist who grew up in rural Maryland and later attended The University of Vermont. He is pursuing his PhD in education studies at UC San Diego, where his work focuses on equity policy, investigating and supporting gender identity development in early childhood, and helping educators to create trans* affirming curriculum, classrooms, and climates. Ben has collaborated with The National Center for Transgender Equality, Trans Family Support Services, Planned Parenthood, Gender Odyssey, San Diego Pride, and others, and has been published in diverse outlets including multiple books, several academic journals, HuffPost, NPR, and more. Ben and his partner Becca have three cats, a three-legged pitbull, and a rotating crew of foster animals. They are passionate about good food, good music, good tattoos, and being good to others.

Dr. Shaylyn Marks (she/her) is an Assistant Professor at CSU Bakersfield and the Director of Multiple and Single Subject Teacher Credential Programs. She received her PhD in English Education from Purdue University in 2013. Dr. Marks was previously a secondary English teacher in Illinois, Indiana, and California before moving to the collegiate level. The main focus of her work centers on advancing innovative ways to disrupt the status quo and create more equitable learning opportunities for underserved populations. With culturally sustaining pedagogy at the core of her work, her research interests include evolving teacher education preparation practices, using literature to support and enact social justice, and exploring equitable structures within the classroom.

Tyrone Martinez-Black (he/they) seeks and solidifies the connections between research, practice, and policy efforts. His current focus is engaging and empowering parents/caregivers to authentically partner with school staff and community members. Tyrone leads an advisory council testing models of shared power amongst adults in homes, schools, and the broader community as co-designers and co-governors of equitable learning environments. Prior to his current work in the field of social and emotional learning, Tyrone taught middle school math and science. He was also an instructional coach and district administrator in those subjects. He began designing and delivering learning experiences for adults during his earliest days as an educator. He continues to do so on a range of topics often intersecting mathematics, equity, and SEL. Tyrone actively collaborates with fellow creatives to generate and elevate models of civic life that offer sovereignty, solidarity, and sustainability for individuals and communities. He strives to honor his immediate family as a grandson, son, husband, and father.

Sharoon Negrete González is a social justice advocate, education researcher, and mentor, committed to advancing community-grounded, affirming, and liberatory educational policies and practices. With expertise in mixed-methods research, program management, and foresight strategy they are currently exploring queer, feminist, and decolonial approaches to schooling, as well as alternative visions and strategies for resistance and resilience through Indigenous and Afrofuturism and youth participatory action research.

Alex Rosado-Torres (he/they) is a genderfluid historian, educator, and activist from Newark, New Jersey. They received their bachelor's degree with honors in history from Rutgers University - New Brunswick and spent time after graduating teaching Middle School English Language Arts in Philadelphia. Currently, they are pursuing their PhD in History of Education & Queer Studies at the University of Illinois Urbana-Champaign where their research is focused on the history of Queer & Trans* activism within educational landscapes in the USA. They are most invested in ensuring that our history continues the work of documenting and preserving Queer & Trans* voices as an act of resistance and love. When they aren't engulfed in education-related work he can be found traveling, practicing the trombone, and testing out new food recipes on his partner, Kevin.

DeKeisha Smith is a special education teacher and will soon start her doctoral studies at the University of North Texas. DeKeisha advocates for and researches ways to make the education system inclusive for foster youth and adoptees. DeKeisha is guided by her lived experiences as a Black, queer, former foster youth throughout her life. The intersectionality of DeKeisha's identity has guided her to the belief that education should lead to liberation for intentionally marginalized communities.

Dr. Mario I. Suárez (he/him) holds a PhD in Curriculum and Instruction from Texas A&M University, an MA in Mathematics Education and a BA in Ethnic Studies from The University of Texas at Austin. He is currently an Assistant Professor in the School of Teacher Education and Leadership at Utah State University. His research interests involve queer and trans* studies in education, STEM retention and persistence, quantitative methods, and curriculum studies.

Jada Thompson (she/her/they), MPH received her master's in public health from The University of Texas Health Science Center School of Public Health, with a focus in Health Promotion and Behavioral Science, along with certificates in Maternal and Child Health and Health Disparities. During their MPH, Jada assisted in research focused on patient and provider engagement involving colorectal cancer screenings in rural Texas, as well as research working with unhoused/recently unhoused populations in Houston by educating them about Hepatitis B and C as well as providing screenings, vaccinations, and treatment. She also worked on research examining the knowledge and perceptions adolescent female patients have towards long-acting reversible contraceptives (LARCs) at the Baylor Teen Health Clinic, where she is currently the Research Coordinator. In their current role, Jada provides comprehensive, evidence-based Abstinence+ sex education to local adolescents in a high school program as well as coordinates immunization events for students who are not up to date on their school-based immunizations.

Dr. B. E. Waid (they/them/elle) is a queer, Latinx, activist-scholar and mathematics coach. They are the founder of the education consulting company, The Queer Mathematics Teacher (QMT). At QMT B. works with pre-service and in-service teachers to rethink and challenge traditional practices in the teaching of mathematics, particularly through the lens of queerness. They are interested in the ways in which students' intersectional identities manifest in mathematical spaces and how to re/humanize mathematics for all students through the use of critical and queer pedagogy. B., along with Dr. Leah Z. Owens, co-founded the Radical Pedagogy Institute, a collective of educators who believe in the transformational power of radical pedagogy and local political organizing. The Institute provides collective members with monthly professional development opportunities on critical, queer, antiracist, and other liberatory pedagogies, as well as opportunities for social and political engagement in New Jersey and New York City. Prior to launching QMT and the Institute, B. worked as an Assistant Professor of Teacher Education, specializing in K-12 mathematics and science. They have also taught middle and high school mathematics in both New York City and Florida. To learn more about B. and their work, visit the QMT website at www.TheQueerMathematicsTeacher.com or the Radical Pedagogy Institute website at www.RadicalPedagogyInstitute.com.

Jay Wang (he/him), MS, MPH earned his degrees, respectively, from The University of North Texas Health Science Center and The University of Texas Health Science Center School of Public Health. Jay has worked in multiple non-profit sectors that range from sexual health, BIPOC mental health, and unstably housed populations. His passions lie in underserved medical communities and developing community-based programming. Jay has participated in projects centered around LGBTQ+ populations, HIV/STI stigma, and substance use. By incorporating aspects of public health and medicine, Jay hopes to continue to address health disparities that exist in The United States at all socio-ecological levels.

Cathery Yeh (she/her) is an assistant professor of Curriculum and Instruction and a core faculty at the Center for Asian American Studies Faculty at The University of Texas at Austin. Her research centers on humanizing teaching practices, ethnic studies, and social justice teaching and organizing. She has been in education for over 20 years, beginning her tenure in dual-language classrooms in Los Angeles and abroad in China, Chile, Peru, and Costa Rica.

INDEX

15-Minute Mindfulness Body Scan, 23
1969 Stonewall Riots, 109
2SLGBTQIA+ community centers, 127–30
    lesson steps for, 130–31, 133–34
    pedagogical notes for, 132–33
    three guiding frameworks for, 134–35

A
About Gender Identity Justice in Schools and Communities, 9
abundance, 37, 56, 66, 77, 103, 124, 134
abundance thinking, 27
action research, 136
Activism: Marsha P. Johnson, 46
Adam, 146
adaptive movement, 21
affirmation, 34
agency, 74
All Boys Aren't Blue, 69
    common core standards for, 70, 78
    lesson steps for, 72–77
    pedagogical notes for, 71–72
    three guiding frameworks for, 77–78
allyship, 51
    common core standards and, 52
    concept of, 53–54
    learning objectives for, 52
    lesson steps for, 53–56
    three guiding frameworks for, 56–57
alt text, 21
American Civil Liberties Union, 5, 13
Anderson, L.H., 102
Annie's Plaid Shirt, 51, 52
    lesson steps for, 53–56
    three guiding frameworks for, 56–57
anti-Blackness, 39
anti-LGBTQ+ bills, 13
anticipating, 132
authentic selves, 51, 66
    common core standards and, 52
    learning objectives for, 52
    lesson steps for, 53–56
    three guiding frameworks for, 56–57
authenticity, 27, 37, 56, 66, 77, 92

B
Baldwin, J., 13
Ballroom Freedom School, 22, 26
belonging, 63, 129
Black LGBTQ+ students, 8, 11, 39–40
    common core standards for, 41
    historical figures and, 46–47
    identity, culture and, 44–45
    learning objectives for, 40
    lesson steps for, 42–47
    pedagogical notes for, 41
    three guiding frameworks for, 47–48
Black Queer diaspora, 45
Black trans* women, 6
body scan, 22, 27
book bans, 13
Boston marriages, 101
box breathing, 24
brain chemicals, developing, 31–32
    common core standards and, 32–33
    definition of happy chemicals, 34
    lesson steps for, 34–36
    pedagogical notes for, 33
    three guiding frameworks for, 36–38
breathing, 23–24
Bridge to Thriving Framework, 9, 11–12, 27, 37, 47, 56, 66, 77–78, 92, 103–4, 115–16, 124, 134–35, 142

C
California History and Social Science Framework, 87
Cameron, L.R., 112
Chappell, S.V., 6
Chen, E., 7, 92, 96, 142
cis, 2
cisgender heteronormativity, 119
cisheteropatriarchy, 39
civics, 130
Clark, C.M., 3, 5
Collaborative for Academic, Social, and Emotional Learning (CASEL), 128
    five core competencies of, 128
collaborative problem solving, 135
colonialism. *See* Two-Spirit people
Combahee River Collective Statement, 46
coming out of the closet, 81–84
compassion, 63
community, 11–12, 37, 47, 56, 66, 77, 92, 124, 134
    affirming, 85
community building, 21, 53
complex gender identities, 103
complexity, 56, 66, 77, 92
confusion, 129
connecting, 134
Conscious Works, 24

Cost of Identity, The, 26
counter-narratives, 109, 112–13
    definition of, 113
Craffey, B., 112
creative arts, 20
critical awareness, 27
critical consciousness, 37, 56, 57, 66, 77, 92, 103
Critical Race Theory (CRT), 127
criticality, 10, 11, 27, 28, 38, 48, 67, 78, 92, 104, 116, 125, 135
Cullen, M., 146
culture, 44
culture and history, 20

D
Daniels, A., 71, 104, 107, 142
Darling-Hammond, K., 9, 11, 145
Davids, S.B., 51, 52
Davidson, J., 130
Dawes, D., 77
deficit thinking, 39
DOSE (dopamine, oxytocin, serotonin, and endorphins), 33
drag bans, 13
drag pedagogy, 124
Drag Queen Story Hour, 6
drag queens, math lessons and, 119–20
    common core standards for, 120–21
    evaluating learning from, 123–24
    lesson steps for, 121–23
    pedagogical notes for, 121
    three guiding frameworks for, 124–25
Duckworth, S., 42
Dyson, A.H., 39

E
educational survival complex, 42
Ellison, J.M., 46
empathy, 63
English Language Skills, 130
equitable access, 131
Evans-Santiago, B., 7, 145
exit ticket, 25
expert groups, 133

F
female husbands, 97–98
    common core standards for, 98–99
    lesson steps for, 99–103
    three guiding frameworks for, 103–4
Female Husbands: A Trans History, 100
five practices, 133, 134
Five Senses Brainstorm, 76
Flores, B., 20, 26, 45, 89
Food Justice, 130
freedom dreaming, 42
freedom journaling, 39, 41, 42
From Pain Comes Strength, 26

futuristic visioning, 27

G
Gay-Straight Alliances (GSAs), 6
gender affirmation, 7
Gender and Sexuality Alliances (GSAs), 3
gender complex, 47, 92
gender creative, 1
    history and context about, 64, 103
Gender Diversity and LGBTQ Inclusion in K-12 Schools, 6
gender fluidity, 103
gender identity, 125
Gender Identity Complexities Framework, 9–10, 27, 37, 47, 56, 66, 77, 92, 103, 115, 125, 134, 142
gender policing, 2
Genishi, C., 39
Getting Curious, 100
Gino, A., 61, 62
GLSEN, 5
grassroots housing models, 26
Griffin-Gracy, M.M., 102
group work, 21
growth mindset, 129

H
Hamilton, C., 102
Happy, 34
happy chemicals. See brain chemicals
Harris County Public Library, 13
Harrison, D., 112
health, 130
healthy human development, 32
Hill, O., 13
Hips on the Drag Queen go Swish, Swish, Swish, The, 120, 121, 125
    See also drag queens
history, 88, 130
historically responsive literacy, 135
    four tenets of, 116
Historically Responsive Literacy Framework, 9, 10–11, 28, 37–38, 48, 57, 66–67, 78, 92–93, 104, 116, 125, 135, 142
home, collective definition of, 25
home groups, 133
home in our bodies, 19–20
    common core standards and, 20
    guiding frameworks for, 27–28
    learning objectives for, 20
    lesson extensions for, 25–26
    lesson steps for, 21–25
    pedagogical notes for, 21
Hot Mess, Lil Miss, 120, 121, 122, 124
House and Ballroom, 22, 26
House of Tulip, 26
Hughes, D., 25, 47, 54, 78
Human Rights Campaign, 5, 13

INDEX

Hurley, P., 5
hypermasculinity, 119

I
identity, 10, 27, 37, 44–45, 48, 69, 78, 92, 125, 129, 135
identity-affirming communities, 45
identity complexity, 73
identity development, 116
identity mapping, 42–44
intellect, 11, 28, 38, 48, 57, 67, 93, 125, 135
intellectualism, 78, 116
intersectionality, 72, 73, 77, 78

J
James, K., 44, 60, 97, 101
Javits, S., 55, 64, 125
Jenkins, A., 102
Jenkins, K., 3, 5
Jigsaw Method, 132
Johnson, G.M., 69, 74
Johnson, M.P., 46, 77
joy, 11, 28, 38, 48, 57, 78
joyful movement, 120
Julián Is a Mermaid, 33, 35, 36, 37

K
Keenan, H.B., 2, 3, 5, 6, 124
Kelley, R.D.G., 42
Kennedy, B., 36, 76, 131
Ketchum, K.E., 6
kindness graph, 33
King, M.L., Jr., 12
Kosciw, J.G., 5

L
lacking, 134
language arts, 40, 51, 61, 70, 120
learning container, 71, 99, 154
Lewey, R., 23
LGBTQ+
    inclusive curricula for, 13
    State of Emergency for, 13
LGBTQ+ history. See transgender history
LGBTQ+ History Month, 5
life science, 32
lifelong professional learning, 3
Lister, A., 102
literacy skills, 37, 135
living queerly, 6
Lorde, A., 39
Love, B., 42
Luebbert, M., 43, 103, 142

M
male wife, 102
Mangin, M., 2, 3, 4, 5, 6
Manion, J., 100

Marrufo, V., 23
Math in Drag, 13
math skills, 37, 120, 130
Matthews, B., 69, 142
Mayo, C., 2–3, 5, 6
Melissa, 61, 62
    common core standards for, 62
    lesson steps for, 63–66
    pedagogical notes for, 62–63
    three guiding frameworks for, 66–67
Meyer, E.J., 3, 5
Miller, s.j., 5, 9, 56, 115, 125
Miranda, D.A., 87
misrecognition, 115
Mission Project, 8, 87
monitoring, 132
Mora, R.A., 113
Morrison, T., 76
Muhammad, G., 9, 10, 116, 125
multiple identities, 28
Murray, P., 46
music, 120
mutual aid, 26
My Name is Pauli Murray, 46
My Perfect Outfit Handout, 52
My Sistah's House, 26

N
National School Climate Survey, 4
neurochemistry, 32
Newsom, G., 13
Notice and Wonder, 121

O
Olson, K., 3
oppression, 77
oxytocin, 32, 34, 37

P
peer feedback, 133
personal identities, 69, 73, 74
Personal Identity Wheel, 73
personal memoirs, 76
Petrus, J., 41, 45
pleasure, 11–12, 37, 134
practice of connecting, 133
primary sources, 112
prior knowledge, 22, 63, 72, 100, 111
project-based learning, 136

Q
queering
    definition of, 39
    expansiveness, fluidity and, 47

R
radical vision writing/drawing, 22
reading, 40, 51, 61, 69, 120

recognition gap, 115
Regan, P.V., 3, 5
relationship skills, 129
relief, 11–12, 27, 37, 56, 66, 77, 134
resistant identity, 92, 103
responsible decision making, 129
Rice, M., 7, 112
Richardson, L., 6
Roberson, M., 22

S
same-gender-loving students, 8, 11, 39–40
    common core standards for, 41
    identity, culture and, 44–45
    learning objectives for, 40
    lesson steps for, 42–47
    pedagogical notes for, 41
    three guiding frameworks for, 47–48
San Francisco Pride Parade (1993), 85, 112
Santos, K., 13
science skills, 37
school-to-coffin pipeline, 146
schools
    as gendered spaces, 4
    reculturing, 4
    safety and, 119
See, Think, Wonder, 121, 122
selecting, 132
self-assertion, 92
self-awareness, 129
self-definition, 27, 66, 77, 92
self-determination, 92
self-management, 129
selfhood, 11–12, 27, 37, 47, 56, 69, 77, 124, 134, 135
sense of belonging, 129
sequencing, 132
serotonin, 32, 34, 37
Simon, A., 23
simply being, 11–12, 27, 37, 47, 56, 66, 77, 124, 135
skills/skillfulness, 10, 28, 48, 67, 78, 93, 116, 125, 135
Smith, M.S., 132, 133
social awareness, 129
social emotional learning, 20, 32, 61, 66, 70, 128–29
    definition of, 128
    transformative, 128–30
social identities, 69, 74
Social Identity Wheel, 72
social studies, 40, 88, 98
STAR, 115–16
Stars and the Blackness Between Them, The, 41, 45
State of Our Nations, 13
Stein, M.K., 132, 133

Stokes, H., 102
storytelling, 28
Stryker, S., 2, 4, 5, 12, 17
Suárez, M., 5, 6
Sullivan, M.J., 39
surveillance, 2
Sylvia and Marsha Start a Revolution, 46
sympathy, 63

T
T*GC (Trans* and gender creative), 1
    affirming and inclusive culture for, 3–4
    BIPOC people and, 26
    celebrating and affirming, 4–5
    definition of, 1
    discrimination and violence against, 3
    guiding frameworks for, 27–28, 36–38
    history and context about, 64
    pedagogy for students, 1–5
    popular culture and, 3
    robust representation of, 5
Think Pair Share, 24–25, 124
thinking map, 53
Thorne, S., 112
Thriving*, 28, 124
trans*. See T*GC
Trans Housing Coalition, 26
transcription/CC, 21
TRANSformational Lotus, 7
Transformative SEL, 128–30
    constructs of, 135
transgender history, 109
    common core standards for, 110
    lesson steps for, 111–15
    three guiding frameworks for, 115–16
Transgender History Month, 13
Transgender Law Center, 5
Transgender Rights Movement, 116
Trino, 146
true belonging, 103
Two-Spirit people, 87–88
    common core standards for, 88
    lesson steps for, 89–91
    three guiding frameworks for, 92–93

U
Unifix cubes, 121, 123
Universal Design for Learning (UDL), 36

V
Van Ness, J., 100
Valerio, M., 112

W
Waid, B.E., 6, 119, 132
We'wha, 102
What Are You Waiting For?, 7

Wheel of Power/Privilege, 42–43
Williams Institute, 4
Williams, P., 33, 34
Wow, Worry, Wonder Rubric, 110, 114
Wozolek, B., 146
writing, 20

Y
yassifying, 121
    definition of, 121
Yeh, C., 96, 119

Z
Zepeda, V., 51, 135

INDEX

Wheel of Reincarnation, 42, 48
Williams Instrument
Williams, C.T., 3n
Wow Worm (Wooden Rubik), 116, 119
Woodall, K., 13n

W, D, 9, 20

Yesilyurt, 117
Yoshihara, circuit 17
Yule, G., 78, 119

Zygote, V, 71, 135n